Curtly Ambrose
Time to Talk

With Richard Sydenham

Forewords by
Richie Benaud and Steve Waugh

Aurum
Press

Quarto is the authority on a wide range of topics.
Quarto educates, entertains and enriches the lives of
our readers—enthusiasts and lovers of hands-on living.
www.QuartoKnows.com

First published in Great Britain
2015 by Aurum Press Ltd
74–77 White Lion Street
Islington
London N1 9PF
www.aurumpress.co.uk

This paperback edition first published in 2016 by Aurum Press Ltd.

A catalogue record for this book is available from the British Library.

ISBN 978 1 78131 543 9
eBook ISBN 978 1 78131 468 5

1 3 5 7 9 10 8 6 4 2
2016 2018 2020 2019 2017

Typeset in Dante MT by SX Composing DTP, Rayleigh, Essex

Printed and bound by CPI Group (UK) Ltd, Croydon, CR0 4YY

Curtly Ambrose

'There is plenty to read here, from details of his early life in Swetes, as the fourth child of seven whose father disappeared to the Virgin Islands to earn money for the family but never came back, to his time as a supreme bowler in the West Indies side.'

The Cricketer

'A very readable account of a career which has been kept somewhat under wraps over the years. A hole has definitely been filled in recent West Indian cricket history with Sir Curtly's honest thoughts, actions and revelations.'

Association of Cricket Statisticians and Historians

'Curtly Ambrose's autobiography has just the right mix of reflection, forthrightness and lists. Pride, professionalism, privacy and justice are common themes throughout the tome, which discloses enough about Ambrose to dispel the urban legend that alleged "Curtly talks to no man".'

ESPN Cricinfo

Contents

Foreword by Richie Benaud

'Curtly's bowling brilliance in Perth to produce the victory by an innings and twenty-five runs [was] certainly one of the finest performances I have ever witnessed'

'Luck's a fortune' is a phrase with which I've grown up from the time I first played cricket in the backyard of our family home at North Parramatta in Sydney, Australia. As a youngster it neatly summed up for me that, although skill is vital for success, if the luck doesn't run with you, your cricketing life could be full of problems.

Being in the right place at the right time is of great importance. Luck was on my side early in 1993 when the West Indies toured Australia under Richie Richardson's captaincy. In the third Test of the series at the Sydney Cricket Ground I watched one of the greatest innings I have seen when Brian Lara stroked his way to 277.

That drawn game was followed by the 'Australia Day' Test in Adelaide where West Indies won a 'nail-biter' by one run.

Then came Curtly's bowling brilliance in Perth to produce the victory by an innings and twenty-five runs; certainly one of the finest performances I have ever witnessed.

One of the quirks of the Perth ground is the breeze from the outer end, known as 'The Fremantle Doctor'; pacemen and swing bowlers from domestic Sheffield Shield and overseas Test countries have fond memories of the assistance they have received over the years.

So, too, do members of the media because there is always something happening to provide interesting paragraphs for a written story, a radio commentary, or someone working on television where often it is a matter merely of adding a few words to the picture on the screen.

Luck comes in different guises. I was fortunate to be able to play in a New South Wales side at the same time as Ray Lindwall, Keith Miller (who had transferred from Victoria to NSW) and other outstanding pace bowlers. Then I was lucky to be around and commentate on others like Sir Curtly Ambrose.

I have found a good way to judge bowling abilities of those I am watching is to consider how I would have batted against them. With Curtly, I rated him as someone against whom I would have had a great deal of difficulty and I am full of admiration for what he achieved in his splendid career.

He has been a high-class bowler and cricketer.

Good luck Curtly, and well done.

Richie Benaud
Coogee, October 2014

Foreword by Steve Waugh

'Curtly Ambrose – the most complete bowler I played against'

The true greats have that little something extra, the ability to shift into another gear when it matters most – often leading to their team taking control of the match. They have the X-factor and as such are both respected and feared by their opponents.

Curtly Ambrose was the most complete bowler I played against during my eighteen-year international career and the guy who tormented Australian teams more than anyone else. He seemed to revel in being the leader of the pack and assumed the mantle with a natural ease. He was a supreme fast-bowling machine whose languid approach to the crease, while mesmerising to the crowd, was both terrifying and often debilitating for the batsman, as he nervously awaited the impending interrogation. It came in two guises: firstly the technical examination of a batsman's technique upon being confronted by a beautifully balanced yet seemingly jet-propelled rhythmic action that delivered the ball from a perfect wrist position at a speed that required complete attention from the batsman to avoid embarrassment or injury. Each delivery prodded and probed every weakness which, when detected, resulted in a relentless pursuit of one's wicket. I always felt that while Curtly kept his strategies simple, he was always analysing your game and critiquing your technique after each delivery, searching for a 'chink in the armour' that he could then exploit.

If you managed to survive his relentless line and length with exaggerated bounce and movement, or the random throat-seeking missile, you then had to confront the physicality of the man. His presence was, to many, overwhelming, with his towering height, deathly stare and imposing body language, leaving many batsmen unsure of his motives. 'Was he trying to get me out or threaten my very existence?' Either was a real possibility, unless complete focus and attention was given to the task at hand. I found myself juggling both these options after I decided to kick over a hornet's nest during our famous confrontation in Trinidad, when I offered Curtly some unwanted advice. Thankfully, Richie Richardson stepped in and saved me from what could have been an embarrassing conclusion to the confrontation. As usual Curtly had the last laugh, claiming six wickets in the innings on a pitch that offered both bounce and movement which, when added to his skill, made batting near-impossible.

We had another reminder of his skill when he steamrollered us in Perth, capturing seven for one in a spell that rates as one of the greatest of all time. Curtly had the killer instinct and could smell blood in the water and would up the ante to seize the moment for his team, often initiating panic in the opposition.

I loved the challenge of batting against him, for it provided a benchmark for me as to where I was at. To succeed against Curtly meant you had graduated as a Test batsman and all those hours of practice and sacrifice were worthwhile. Quite simply, he was the best I faced and each run scored off him had to be earned and that's exactly how Test cricket was meant to be played. Always 100 per cent!

Steve Waugh,
Sydney, November 2014

Time to Go

'I was fit enough and good enough to have played on for another eighteen months and maybe even two years, but I wanted to leave at the top of my game rather than have people say I should have retired a year ago. My pride is important to me and I know I left cricket at the right time'.

I first wanted to retire during the 1995 tour of England. I reconsidered my future and decided it wasn't the right time for me or West Indies cricket then – I will expand on this later in the book. I felt more serious about retirement at the start of 1998. We had a tour of Pakistan in late '97 that we lost badly, 3-0. I missed the last match of that series with a slight back strain and since the series was gone there wasn't much point in me aggravating my back. So after that tour I thought to myself, 'It's time to finish with this cricket thing.' I started to lose interest, the passion wasn't there any more and I didn't feel like going on. My plan was to play one last season with the Leeward Islands and try to win the domestic championship, finish on a high, and then call it a day, which would have meant not playing in the England series at the start of 1998. So I was set on retirement with West Indies.

However, I would not want to get into name-calling but during that domestic season there were a few commentators who were suggesting that Curtly Ambrose was all washed up, mainly because of my poor performance in Pakistan. While these criticisms were going around I started to reconsider whether I wanted to bow out on such a negative note. But still, I was set on going ahead with my retirement plans. In fact, while the Leeward Islands were in Barbados I asked a very good friend of mine, Roland Holder, to help me draft a retirement letter that I would send to the West Indies Cricket Board. Roland confidentially told a very good friend of his about my intended letter and his friend just happened to be a newspaper reporter. This guy wasn't able to keep the secret and broke the news to the world that Curtly Ambrose was retiring from cricket. I then started getting calls from all over and I had to deny the story because it wasn't the way I wanted my retirement to be handled. I have always been very professional and I wanted to go out the right way, which was to inform the West Indies board of my retirement before the media or anyone else. Although the rumour getting out didn't change my feelings on retirement, I had two things eating away at me. One, I was irritated by the negative comments saying that I was over the hill and the competitor in me wanted to prove them wrong. And two, I wanted my employers to know about my intentions before the whole world. It was a messy situation and I didn't feel good about it so I thought, 'No, I'm going to continue and show that Curtly Ambrose still has a lot of cricket left in him.' I wanted to finish when *I* planned, not the media or anyone else.

That ugly episode allowed me to acknowledge that my interest in the game was still there. In trying to get out of cricket, I inadvertently rediscovered my drive and motivation, thanks to my critics. They helped give me another three years with the West Indies. I have always thrived on criticism. My pride is everything to me so it was important I carried on and finished when I was comfortable about going.

What was interesting, even though I had decided to carry on, the selectors picked six fast bowlers in the squad for the first Test against England in Jamaica – the ill-fated game that was abandoned. Although I will speak about that match later, I want to make the point that such an unprecedented selection of *six* fast bowlers for a Test was a clear sign that the selectors had concerns as to whether myself and possibly Courtney Walsh were still good enough to carry on at the top level. You might see six fast bowlers in tour squads but never before had six quicks featured in a squad for a home Test. Five, maybe, but never six. The rumours were flying about but my mind was made up that I was carrying on and I know Courtney also had no plans to bow out at that stage. It was a good decision as the Leeward Islands came first, albeit jointly with Guyana, and it also allowed me to address my loss of interest in the game. It never had anything to do with financial aspects; it was purely about cricket and my acknowledgement that my passion wasn't there any more. I had fallen out of love with the game. And I am such a professional that if I ever feel I cannot give 100 per cent, I would prefer not to do it. But that passion returned when people suggested I was all washed up.

Fast forward to May 2000 and I was ready to retire once again. This time, it was during a home series with Pakistan. Before the third Test started in my homeland of Antigua, I confided in Courtney Walsh, as we were not just bowling partners, we were (and still are) like brothers – really close. There was never any rivalry between us – ever. If it was his day to take wickets then my job was to just keep the pressure on at the other end. If it was my day, he would do the same thing. So I told him that game was going to my last and he immediately protested and said I had to carry on. I would keep asking him, 'Why should I continue?' And at the end of the Test match, which we won by one wicket, he said: 'I will give you one reason why you have to carry on. You *have* to reach 400 [Test wickets].' I was on 388 after that series and to be honest, stats never meant much to me and I was happy to go then and finish on 388. But Cuddy kept banging on to me how I had to join my partner in the 400 Club. As well as Courtney, there was only Kapil Dev, Richard Hadlee and Wasim Akram. Although plenty of others have since reached that milestone, I will always be the fifth who got there so I am really glad I carried on. I had always played my cricket for the team throughout my career, never for myself. But on this occasion I thought, 'Cuddy's got a point, 400 would be quite nice. It would be very special to be in a club of just five.' So I carried on and went to England, but not before I gave a press conference in the Caribbean saying that I would retire after the England tour. There it was. Officially, the secret was out. There was no more backing out of retirement. First my critics motivated me out of it in '98 and now my big buddy Courtney Walsh had talked me out of it in 2000. But I was very comfortable that my West Indies career would be no more after the fifth Test against England at The Oval.

That final match was just like any other for me, it didn't feel any different. My fiancée Bridget (who became my wife the following year) was over with my two daughters. My eldest girl, Tanya, would have been ten and Chloe two. We have since added two more daughters. We had a relaxed family dinner the night before the final day of that fifth Test and it all felt normal. Having my family around would have helped me, for sure. I slept very well, I wasn't nervous, I never had any regrets and I was completely comfortable that it was all about to end. I just wanted to go home and relax and put my feet up and live my life. My retirement never had anything to do with the team's decline and results. It's true we were not playing as well as we used to, but if I wanted to get out because of results then I would have left long before this time. I stayed on because I thought I could still make a contribution to West Indies cricket. Even at this time I was confident I was fit enough and good enough to have played on for another eighteen months and maybe even two years, but I wanted to leave at the top of my game rather than have people say I should have retired a year ago. My pride is important to me and I know I left cricket at the right time.

Besides, the international cricket treadmill was starting to take its toll and I was feeling like I wanted to sleep longer in the mornings. I am a breakfast person: I love my breakfast and for too many mornings on that tour I had missed breakfast because I stayed longer in bed and had to rush straight out of the hotel on to the team bus for the match or practice. Every time I played on that tour I gave 100 per cent after the bell rang, but on the field or during intervals I'd be looking at my watch and thinking, 'I can't wait for six o'clock', or 'God, is it only three o'clock, I want it to be six.' It was becoming a challenge to carry on. Those were signs that it was definitely time to go and give someone else a chance. But I was pleased my good friend Courtney Walsh convinced me to go to England and get to 400. There are very few people in this world who are able to convince me to do something that I don't want to do, but Courtney did it then, and I'm pleased he did.

That fifth day at The Oval was also a very normal day. Through the tour I had got used to Bridget waking me up in the morning and saying, 'Don't you have to be on the bus soon?' And I would sleep a little longer and dash to the bus. I am not one for any grand farewells or fanfare so we travelled to the ground as normal; there were no special words or awards. It was simply business as usual. We were 33 for no wicket overnight, chasing 374 to win. Although history tells us we were bowled out for 215 to lose the game heavily and the series by 3-1, I began that Monday morning expecting us to win the game, as I started every day of Test cricket in my career. I am a very confident person and even if my team was behind the eight ball I always felt we could pull things around, especially with the ball. I can maybe only give you twenty or thirty with the bat, but with the ball I always felt we could defend anything. So losing never entered my mind at the start of play, not until we were several wickets down. I am a realist so I then knew the game was gone. I was heartened, though, when England gave me a guard of honour as I walked out to bat, in front of a packed Oval crowd who all stood and applauded me. It was a nice gesture and it caught me by surprise as I had never seen it before. I'd had some battles with the England guys over the years – in county and international cricket – and that gesture meant they appreciated and respected my contribution to cricket. That was very heart-warming.

I also figured, in a more fun way, they were clapping my farewell because they were glad to see the back of me. Some – not me – would say Mike Atherton more than most. And I know people say Atherton was my bunny as I dismissed him seventeen times in Test cricket. But I have never looked at it that way as he scored a lot of runs against us as well, like in this match at The Oval (83 and 108). He was a decent player. As an opening batsman you are always facing the new ball when the bowlers are fresh; it's never an easy task. I always had respect for him. While he was not the most talented of cricketers I've seen he was certainly a fighter. It is a difficult job being an opening batsman, yet he had a wonderful career. But going back to the guard of honour, it was an appreciation of my work and it made me feel good about myself and my career. It was emotional actually but I didn't shed any tears. Being an aggressive person by nature I would not have wanted to shed a tear then – the England guys might have thought I was going soft!

The dressing room was quiet after the game. The guys knew me too well to be foolish enough to plan any party or celebration straight after losing the match and the series. It was even more painful a defeat after we had won the first Test inside three days at Edgbaston only to then lose a tight game at Lord's and hand England the initiative, which they never let go of. If we had won at The Oval to square the series then maybe there might have been a small celebration for me, but I was in no mood to have fun after this result. The guys knew me too well to try and arrange anything.

It was a sad way to end my career, but at least I am able to say I ended the way I started, with a defeat!

As a man who became almost as famous for saying nothing as for taking wickets, some might ask 'Why now?' Why tell your life story fifteen years after you retired? The simple answer is 'the time feels right'. I believe it's time to lift the lid on the unique culture of West Indies cricket that I knew and what it was like to be part of the West Indies team from my debut in 1988 through to 2000, and even beyond to my coaching days more recently. It has been an eventful journey from the days of world domination in the late eighties and mid-nineties, and then through to more challenging times.

The Early Years

'Sometimes Mum would go without food, putting her children first before herself when times were especially tough. We children never went without and for that we owe Mum a great deal'

Life for me began in Swetes, a vibrant community with a population of around 1,800 and 11km from the hustle and bustle of Antigua's capital, St John's. Back then in the 1960s, it was a close-knit, proud neighbourhood where everyone knew everyone and all looked out for one another. Swetes was viewed by the more judgemental city types as something of an outpost stuck in south central Antigua that was never realistically going to produce a cricketer of any repute – certainly not a Test cricketer! But cricket was an integral part of the village culture, even if football has overtaken it in more recent times. I was raised with an ingrained respect for my people and if anyone would ever suggest one needed to play outside Swetes to be more ambitious, we were soon advised otherwise. Maurice Francis, an old boss of mine who became a long-time friend, told me, 'If you're good enough you will be noticed anywhere. They will find you in Barters!' That was an Antiguan village even more remote than Swetes. The great Andy Roberts left his fishing village home in Urlings to play for Rising Sun in St John's, but that was more to do with the best competition recruiting the best players. We felt, in Swetes, that we could compete with the best. So I remained and never regretted it, even though I was to face my share of prejudices – at home and elsewhere around the Caribbean.

My journey began on 21 September 1963. I was born to Hillie Otto and Joshua Ambrose and was the fourth child of seven. My mother insisted there would have been many more of us if my father had not migrated to the US Virgin Islands and, latterly, New Jersey in the US. Mum and Dad were married on 26 July 1956 and according to my elder siblings were a happy couple. But it was not uncommon for working men in Antigua to go off in search of better prospects that would ease the financial burden back home. The US Virgin Islands was a regular pathway to the States, as visas were not needed from there. Once Dad had made that shift when I was still a baby, the children became my mother's responsibility. First there was my big sister Anesta, the eldest child; then my elder brother Aldansa (or Danny to everyone else), then came Alicia and me next, to keep the girl-boy-girl-boy pattern going. For some reason Mum ran out of names beginning with 'A' and I was named Curtly Elconn Lynwall. I don't know why the first two but Lynwall stemmed from Mum's passion for cricket, after the great Australian fast bowler Ray Lindwall, even if the spelling is a little different! After me followed Ophelia, Willysteen – who opted for her second name of Heidi because they spelt her first name wrong on the birth certificate, and my kid brother Jamie was the seventh sibling.

I suppose I was renowned throughout my career as a fast bowler who never shirked long spells or hard labour on flat wickets. I would imagine that work ethic was handed down in the genes from those before me. Mum's father, Archiebald Otto, was a pipefitter for the Antiguan Public Works and her mother, Henrietta David, was a fruit farmer. Dad's father was a fisherman. My father, who was commonly known as Jasper, was a labourer at a sugar cane factory near home. He was later a carpenter. No one, though, worked harder than my mother, who became the single most influential figure in my young life and into adulthood. Once Dad took off for the US Virgin Islands she was left alone to keep all seven of us fed and watered and I must say she managed to do just that, quite heroically. Mum would walk half an hour every morning into the hills to struggle on her hands and knees picking potatoes for a local farmer. That job gave her a modest wage but enough to ensure her children had food on the table every day. She would bring home a small amount of money plus the perks of her occupation, a handful of potatoes. Anesta told me that sometimes Mum would go without food, putting her children first when times were especially tough. We children never went without and for that we owe Mum a great deal. We also owe our Christian faith to Mum, who was very religious and encouraged us to go to church. Church was almost as much a part of society in Swetes as cricket. I still go now whenever I am home.

Dad had initially left Swetes with good intentions to better himself and, in turn, his income, which was supposed to provide for his family and make things easier for Mum and all of us back home. He landed a job with the oil refinery, Hess, in St Croix. Occasionally he would return home on leave and the first time that happened I didn't know who he was because I hadn't seen him before (he'd left when I was a baby). As time passed the food parcels and money he'd send from the US Virgin Islands started to dry up and eventually stopped. Dad was a smoker, a heavy drinker and gambled much of his earnings, so that wouldn't have left much for the family back home. We didn't really grow up with our father a lot. However, we all went to visit him in St Croix at times – I went there once with Danny when I was seven or eight. That was the time I started to get to know him. After that I didn't see him again until 1988 when I was almost twenty-five. I only saw him then because West Indies went to New York to play two exhibition games after the 1988 tour of England. Even though I hadn't seen him for seventeen or eighteen years and hadn't even spoken on the phone to him either, we still connected. Dad never saw me play for West Indies apart from those two games in New York when Danny brought him down. I was pleased to see him and he was happy to see me. He always called me 'Big Boy'. We were all tall in the family – my Dad was 6ft 2in, Danny is 6ft 4in and Jamie's about 6ft 1in. Looking back, we just got used to not having Dad around. Mum was our tower of strength. Danny and two of my sisters, who all live in New Jersey, knew him much better after Dad relocated to the US.

Even though Dad was not part of our lives growing up, we still loved him. Whenever we had a chance to see him there was no animosity or hard feelings. Most kids who grow up without their father being around despise their dad. But that wasn't the case with us. We're a close family and Mum made sure we were there for one another. It says a lot about Mum that although she was left on her own for so many years she never once dirtied his name, which is why the children never stopped loving him. No matter how hard life became for her – and it was hard – she never held it against my dad. And we would ask her a lot, 'Where's Daddy? Why he never around? Why he not support you?' She never once gave him a bad name so we grew up thinking he was a good man. The only negative things she spoke of were his gambling, smoking and drinking and she told us only because she did not want us to do these things. Dad wasn't what you might call a drunk; he didn't go falling all over the place, but he did drink quite heavily and Mum said he wasn't the same man when he drank. He did that from the early days in Antigua, but I understand he became worse when he left home. From listening to my mum speak on these things, it had an influence on me. I grew up a non-smoker and non-drinker. I tasted alcohol once or twice, when the West Indies boys persuaded me to try some champagne or beer, but I hated it! I do have the odd Bailey's but I don't regard that as beer or hard liquor.

My dad passed away in 1989, aged just fifty-nine. It was too young for him to be taken from us. Curiously, he always looked on doctors with deep suspicion, though I never did get to the bottom of why that was so. It should not have come as any surprise then – on being told by a doctor in the hospital that he would require surgery to preserve his life – that he died the night before surgery was due to take place. Maybe it was the way he would have wanted it. He had internal complications but I take some comfort that he died peacefully. I am just pleased I had the opportunity to spend some time with him the year before.

As far as Mum goes, she has always been and still is a cricket fanatic. I remember from when I was a boy she would have a little transistor radio and listen to the cricket all hours of the day and night. I suppose that would be my first introduction to cricket. Not that it made much of an impression on me but it was always there. She would go on about 'Sobers, The Three Ws, Kanhai, Lloyd coming up'. It would actually annoy me because I wanted to know about basketball, not cricket. I'd say to her, 'Mum, I can't understand what fun you get from this cricket commentary!' She steered me towards cricket at any possible opportunity. If we were in town and there was a cricket match on – it didn't have to be West Indies or the Leeward Islands but maybe only a club match – she would stay and watch and make me watch it too. Not that I appreciated it all that much, as cricket never really interested me until I was nearer twenty – even then I still didn't love it. I only played cricket because everyone else in Swetes played it. If you were male and not involved with cricket in Swetes, then it would not be difficult to be something of a social outcast.

In my earlier days when I was six or seven I had more fun playing marbles. We had a mango tree in our backyard but in the front garden there was a guinep tree – which is still there to this day, actually – and friends from around the neighbourhood would come over to my place to do battle with their marbles right by that guinep tree. The yard was like a dusty, dried patch of dirt and you could roll your marbles on the ground. The game was to draw a triangle on the ground with a stick and if there were six of us playing then the first person decided on how many marbles he set inside that triangle – typically it would be three, maybe four – and then the other guys had to place the same amount inside. You then took it in turns rolling a slightly bigger marble to see how many you could bump outside the triangle. If you managed to move at least one out of it, you went again until you missed. However many marbles you moved outside you kept – they were your winnings. I would say, as funny as it sounds, that game started my competitive spirit as it could be quite serious – everybody wanted to win badly.

If Mum tried hard to pique my interest in cricket and failed, my brother Danny was more successful, albeit in a forceful, big brother way. Danny was widely respected throughout Antigua as a wicketkeeper-batsman and if our family was to produce a West Indies cricketer everyone thought it would be Danny. In my mid-teen years Danny 'persuaded' me to umpire the Swetes Village league matches. I was known to score the odd game, too. Cricket up to then was just something to do, pretty much; also at Swetes Primary School and then at All Saints Secondary School and at home in the road in front of my house. It was a way of remaining a member of the in-crowd. I enjoyed basketball more but if you didn't play cricket you felt left out.

School friend and future West Indies team-mate Winston Benjamin recalled: 'I first met Curtly at All Saints Secondary School. There were lots of little cliques and he was part of the school cricket team clique so although he wasn't bothered by cricket he was encouraged to play. To start with at about thirteen, fourteen he was bowling some gentle medium pace – he wouldn't have killed ants with the pace he was bowling. After school he didn't gravitate towards cricket and was more into basketball and later was an ardent footballer in our Premier Division. He was the Patrick Vieira-type midfield player – only he didn't tackle! His brother Danny, though, was different. I was at the primary school when Danny was in secondary and I'm telling you he was one of the finest keepers I've ever seen – in the Jeffrey Dujon mould. Once a ball went into his gloves it never came out. He had a lot of influence on Curtly, though his mum was also a very ardent cricket fan.'

I wouldn't say I liked school; it was just something I had to do, though once I was at All Saints Secondary I really didn't care for chemistry and physics too much. All those test tube bottles and what I called funny language. I was never a great student but I got by, although after passing the first form at All Saints I started to slacken off and waste time. Mum would keep telling me to study but I didn't give the school books enough attention and before I knew it I was forced to repeat second form while my friends advanced to third form. I passed second form, went up to third form and started to fool around again and was made to repeat third form. So by the time my friends had completed fifth form, I had only finished third form. By then aged seventeen I wasn't prepared to go through another two years of school when I should have been starting college like my friends. So I decided to quit school, find a job and help my mother to put food on the table. She wasn't happy about it – in fact she was highly annoyed – but after some time she understood where I was coming from and gave me her blessing to find a job. I felt I had to contribute at home when Mum's struggle to keep us all fed and clothed was so obvious. I must say, though, there was one thing that made the Ambrose family quite special in Swetes from the late 1960s. We were one of the few houses in my area that had a TV set. They were scarce. Mum came back from St Croix one time with this portable black and white television. She couldn't have afforded to buy one in Antigua – we felt like we were top of the world. Our neighbours would congregate at our house to watch shows on it with us. My favourite was *Gunsmoke* – I grew up loving westerns and still do. I enjoyed Chinese karate movies also but westerns were my favourite: with John Wayne, Clint Eastwood, Henry Fonda, Charles Bronson – these guys were my favourites. I still watch the DVDs now – I love them.

My first job was in a clothing store but I didn't like it much, I didn't think it was *manly* enough. So I stayed there for maybe three months. I wanted a more *manly* job and looked for a trade. I eventually became a carpenter because a good friend of mine was a mason and he helped me find a job with the government, the Antiguan Public Works. I was sent to work as an apprentice mason in Urlings as they were building a school there. But on arrival, it was clear there was no work for masons so I told them I was there to work as a carpenter as I didn't want to go home – I was there to work and earn. I worked as a carpenter from 1981 to 1984, when I started playing for Swetes.

I tried several jobs like masonry, carpentry and then changing tyres at a garage in Swetes, which was a job I enjoyed because my friend Ballu was there. His real name is Keithroy Robinson but he's always been known as Ballu as long as I can remember, since we were together at Swetes Primary School (now the Irene B. Williams School). I used to walk past this garage most days with friends from my neighbourhood on our way to pick coconuts. On a Saturday or Sunday morning my friends used to take me to get some fresh coconut water, or jelly as we call it Antigua, to prime me up for the cricket match over the weekend. You drink the sweet water and then cut it open to eat the fruit. That was our routine as the guys felt that got me going for the cricket. I'd go and help Ballu out, at first just casually, but after a while they gave me a job because the mason and construction work took a lot of energy out of me, which was no good for my cricket. The tyre-changing job was less taxing on my body. The first time I did it I told Ballu, 'I've been watching you changing those tyres for weeks. I think I can do that.' Ballu suggested it wasn't as easy as it looked but he gave me a go as I was always up for a challenge. If anyone told me I couldn't do something I'd want to prove them wrong. So I had a go and managed half of it; I was almost there but not quite. Eventually the boss, Maurice Francis, gave me a job.

> Garage owner Maurice Francis added, on the honest nature of young Curtly:
> 'I was doing some bookkeeping one day and found that Curtly's takings were over – not under but over. I approached him about it and he told me that people gave him three dollars extra here and two dollars extra there. I explained to him that money was a tip for him to put into his own pocket. He knew it but rather than be accused of stealing he preferred to add those tips to the overall takings. That sums up just how honest the boy was.'

The first time I started to take cricket seriously was for the Swetes Village team when I was aged twenty. I came into cricket reluctantly in 1984. But I am a proud man and if I was going to do something I was going to do it to the best of my ability. My mother pretty much forced me into playing cricket and I didn't want to disappoint her. As I've said, at that time I only wanted to play basketball. I never wanted to play cricket because I never 'loved' it. People say to me, imagine how good you could have been if you had 'loved' cricket. But my take is, if I had loved cricket, I would have thought about it too much and I would have been worse. As it was, I knew when to switch on and off. Once I stepped over the rope I put my game face on. When I came off the field I didn't want to speak about cricket or even hear about cricket. Desmond Haynes used to tell me that I was a freak with the way I was able to switch on and off. But going back, Mum was the driving force behind my cricket because she was a cricket freak and was actually a good player herself. She tells me she used to beat on the boys at cricket when she was young.

I might have started playing serious cricket slightly earlier than twenty if Swetes had not been decimated by selections for the Parish Representative XI, which meant we had no team for three years. That was the time my brother Danny became frustrated with cricket and left for the US. In those barren years for Swetes, though, we started an out-of-season five-team competition amongst ourselves, played with a tennis ball because the grounds were quite small. I played for Vicarage, which had its ground about two minutes from my house. There was also St Ann's (who named their ground 'Lord's' because it was the largest of Swetes' playing areas), Norfolk (who called their ground the 'Gabba' after the Brisbane arena), Corner (or 'Perth') and Roman Hill. That competition lasted only three years until Swetes returned to the local league but it spawned a more official national softball cricket tournament that still runs to this day. So we were innovators in Swetes! In fact I learned to bowl properly with a tennis ball when aged seven or eight. People used to comment that I had a very good, conventional action at an age when other kids were chucking. During school holidays we also played matches that were known as 'pick-a-side'. That was as the name suggests: two captains taking it in turns to pick a side with all the players lined up. It wasn't unusual in the earlier days for yours truly to be one of the last to be picked. And back then I fancied myself more as a batsman. Because we played with tennis balls you faced a lot of bouncers so you learned how to hook. As I got older, though – and taller – it became apparent to all that my bowling was going to be my strong suit. Early mentors like Enoch Lewis, who was something of a star in Swetes as he played for the Leeward Islands, and Malverne Spencer, who was the Swetes team manager and chief administrator, were forever encouraging me to bowl more, having identified some talent in me.

My cricket began to attract serious interest through my performances in the local Parish League, Division Two, which saw games played over a whole weekend. We played teams from the St Paul parish and other local sides, which included Liberta, New Winthropes, Buckley's, Falmouth, Freetown and All Saints. This was hard-ball cricket and there were serious bragging rights at stake. I was now twenty; yes, a late developer but progressing quickly. When we returned to league action in 1984 I had become a part of the team. I bowled well but for some reason had become the subject of rumours that I was unable to bowl a second spell. That wasn't true; it was rubbish talk and was my first experience of cricket politics in my region. There were plenty more political hurdles ahead to clear. This was just the first. How can you play cricket every week and only have one spell? I was the main bowler in the Swetes team so where those stories came from was a mystery.

My breakthrough year was 1985, but I nearly didn't play at all that year. The cricket boots that I used in 1984 had worn out and were unwearable. I said to myself, 'No cricket for me this year' because I couldn't afford to be spending my precious few dollars on a new pair of cricket boots as I'd rather use that money to go to the cinema and watch westerns or something like that. But the Swetes manager Malverne Spencer said to me, 'You have a future in cricket, I will buy your boots.' And he went ahead and bought a pair of size 14 boots for me with his own money so that I could play. I have never forgotten it and it's possible that if I hadn't played for Swetes in 1985 with those new boots I might never have had a cricket career, as that is where my journey began.

Swetes won the double in 1985, beating Barnes Hill in the one-day competition and Pigotts in the two-day tournament – both games were at the Antigua Recreation Ground (ARG), for my first taste of cricket at that Test venue, which was a special moment for me. That match against Pigotts didn't start well for me. The very first ball of the game I was cut for four and even then I hated giving runs away. I got vexed. Enoch Lewis sensed my mood and ran to me from slip and asked, 'What are you going to do now?' I told him I was going to bowl a bouncer and try to knock off the batsman's head. He calmed me down, explained to me that the batsman would be expecting the short ball and convinced me to bowl a yorker, while pushing two fielders back on the fence for the double bluff. The tactic worked and I sent his stumps flying. I was still a rookie and was happy to listen to Enoch. It was a good early lesson about the need to think about my bowling; I finished with seven wickets and it was instrumental in me getting picked for Antigua that year.

Enoch Lewis recalled: 'Curtly's special talent was the rib-cage ball that got big on batsmen off a good length. There was no team around who could survive against Curtly and his fellow fast bowler Oswald Steele. Curtly gave a lot of pride and hope to the people of Swetes. So many people would turn out and watch on the weekends. Swetes became so dominant with Curtly in the team.'

Swetes had given me all that I needed to that point, but because of my late development I needed to progress quickly and the national team was the next target. Fortunately, my achievements with my village had put me on that path. I made my debut for Antigua & Barbuda on 8 June 1985 against St Kitts at the ARG and here I found myself rubbing shoulders for the first time with the great Andy Roberts, who had been persuaded to play to add experience to a young team despite already ending his distinguished West Indies career. I was picked ahead of Vaughn 'Hungry' Walsh to line up alongside Kenny Benjamin, Jenson Joseph and Andy Roberts, who had enjoyed legendary status in Antigua for as long as I could remember and it was a privilege to be his team-mate. I hadn't received much in the way of coaching so to then suddenly find myself taking advice from a guy like Andy was quite inspiring. That game couldn't have gone any better for me, with figures of seven for 67, ten for 126 in the match, from my seventeen overs after coming on first change. St Kitts had been 82 for no loss but were eventually bowled out for 241. It was another giant leap for me, though as I neared selection for the Leeward Islands – the last stop before representing West Indies – I soon discovered that if I was to achieve anything in this game I would have to do it the hard way and would face many obstacles. I quickly learned that playing cricket at the top in the West Indies can be a bumpy ride.

Says Andy Roberts: 'That Antigua game was my last competitive match and Curtly's first. We had a lot in common as I also came from a remote village where nobody looked for cricketers. I know exactly what he went through. In those days he bowled two lengths: full and short. I remember thinking to myself, the day this guy finds a length of his own, which he eventually did, he will be a world beater.'

A Reluctant Cricketer

*'Even when on the verge of the West Indies team, I still didn't like
cricket. I played it and persevered with it because people I respected told
me I was good at it. If I'd followed my own dreams I would have been
going off to the US and signing for an NBA team'*

My mother's dreams were realised when I was selected to make
my first-class debut for the Leeward Islands on 12 February 1986.
She was already proud of me before I made a name for myself
because I played for Swetes and Mum just wanted a cricketer in
the family – at any level. When my big brother left for the US
and abandoned his promising cricket career, you could say the
baton passed to me. By early 1986, my cricket career was taking
off quickly. Those close to me were adamant it was only a matter
of time before West Indies selection followed. The truth is, even
at this stage of my career with so much going right for me, I still
didn't like cricket. I played it and persevered with it because
people I respected told me I was good at it. If I'd followed my
own dreams I would have been going off to the US and signing

for an NBA team, via college basketball. The American influence on TV in Antigua is very strong and probably somewhere around the mid-seventies I got hooked on basketball because it seemed very exciting. I first started playing at All Saints Secondary School because they had a concrete court there and it allowed me to hone my skills. I wouldn't say I was great but I could handle myself (as a centre) and would later play for Swetes in the Antigua league for many years, even after I retired from the West Indies team. In fact I played during my West Indies career, even football from 1995, at the height of my cricket powers. If it was up to me I would have continued playing basketball and football throughout my cricket career but in the end the Swetes villagers refused to register my name for the leagues because they felt I should focus more on my cricket. I was highly annoyed at the time but I quickly realised they were right; they acted with my best interests in mind.

West Indies and Antigua legend Andy Roberts commented: 'I heard Curtly say over the years that he doesn't like cricket but I cannot see how someone can improve so much if they do not "love" cricket. I always thought he was kidding himself; yes, he liked basketball but he must have loved cricket to be so intense all the time in his bowling. Pride was a big part of his game but that doesn't come without love.'

My passion for basketball started with the Philadelphia 76ers as I liked Dr J (Julius Erving). He was my first real hero. I never idolised cricketers, it was always basketball players. Charles Barkley later joined the 76ers and I liked him as well. As Dr J retired I began to slide away from the 76ers and support the

Atlanta Hawks because I was a huge fan of Dominique Wilkins. After a number of years I moved away from the Hawks and supported the Phoenix Suns because Charles Barkley moved there. Later I started supporting Tim Duncan at the San Antonio Spurs. I took a break for a few years then and didn't support a team. But more recently I have been following Oklahoma City Thunder as I like Kevin Durant. They're a young team and I always back the underdog. It might be a surprise that I haven't mentioned Michael Jordan or Magic Johnson but everyone wants to support the Bulls or the Lakers as they are great teams. Even though I never supported either of those champion teams, I always admired Michael Jordan and Magic Johnson as great players, but I prefer to support a team that is on its way up. So when they win a Championship I can say I was there with them from the start!

I was not part of the original Leeward Islands attack in '86 when Eldine Baptiste, Tony Merrick, Winston Benjamin and George Ferris were in ahead of me. Unfortunately for Merrick and Ferris they got injured before the Guyana game, our final match of the Shell Shield campaign. Since I had performed well for Antigua they drafted me in for that game – not that I was exactly over the moon. The call-up came over the phone while I was at the tyre garage. I wasn't all that interested in going as I still didn't care about cricket. My boss, Maurice Francis, was happier for me than I was and he persuaded me to go and play. That was my first experience of first-class cricket and the Leeward Islands. I flew over to Georgetown separately to join up with the guys for my initial glimpse of first-class cricket and playing for the Leeward Islands. Crucially, it also meant a first meeting with the great Viv Richards, who had never seen me bowl.

Meeting Viv, a hero in Antigua, for the first time wasn't the intimidating experience some might think. The fact I had people around me who I was already familiar with made it easier. There was my close friend from school, Winston Benjamin, my cousin Ralston Otto and one of my early mentors from Swetes, Enoch Lewis, so it was not like I had to walk into a totally alien dressing room before meeting up with Viv. It was not at all nerve-racking. I had no preconceived expectations, though I knew about him and his reputation as a player, but I soon discovered he ran a very relaxed dressing room and liked to have a laugh and a joke and a bit of fun. Viv is the most passionate cricketer you could meet on the field, but in the dressing room he enjoys a relaxed approach. On the field he was a very tough leader for whom winning was everything. He hated seeing guys just going through the motions. These high standards that he demanded meant that it came naturally for his players to follow his example, and it was easy to raise your own game. If you weren't doing the job he expected of you, he would let you have it. And thankfully I was only on the receiving end a few times, when he felt I slipped below my high standards. Those moments were never pleasant as Viv would use some colourful language and a few choice words. But he was a fair man and would never chastise anyone for nothing. If he was preparing to give you a piece of his mind, he would always inquire first, 'Are you OK?' just in case you were ill or injured. It was his way of eliminating any excuses before he let rip. Viv was very straightforward and I enjoyed playing under his captaincy because we're both highly competitive. He welcomed me to the team and made it easy for me to feel part of things pretty quickly, and encouraged me a lot out in the middle. I took four wickets in the game (two in each innings) and Viv was rather impressed. It was inspiring when he said to me in front of the guys afterwards, 'Where have you been hiding?' He also spoke to me, even at that early stage, about what I needed to do to play for the West Indies. His advice was more about character than anything too technical, touching on the importance of professionalism, self-belief, total commitment and, of course, pride. It was heartening to feel his support at such a time in my career.

The year 1986 was also when I left the Caribbean for the first time. I played for Chester Boughton Hall in the Liverpool & District League. A gentleman by the name of Geoff Moss organised it in conjunction with the Viv Richards Scholarship scheme. Maybe I should have been excited about this opportunity to go and experience life in a different country but the truth is I had no interest in going. And then Maurice convinced me. Coming from a hot Caribbean country I was worried about what I had heard of the cold weather in England. But Mr Francis said, 'Just take the plane ride and experience England and come home if you don't like it, but at least go.' Winston Benjamin had been on the same scholarship the year before. It was my first trip outside the Caribbean and, not knowing anyone, it was hard for me at first. The club treated me well but I was seriously homesick. My feelings were, 'I can't deal with this cold, it's not for me, I gotta go back.' I never quite got used to that cold. I didn't want to leave the house – it was freezing! But I toughed it out and bowled well, took 84 wickets (at an average of 9.80).

'He went there and created a storm,' Swetes team manager Malverne Spencer remembers. 'We would have reports of his performances sent to us in Antigua and I had them broadcast on the radio. Ambrose was receiving a lot of hype.'

Winston took over a hundred the year before so he reminded me about that quite often. Fortunately, in terms of getting back at Winston, I returned in '87 and took 115 wickets for Heywood in the Central Lancashire League so I was able to have my revenge on him. That was the season when Northamptonshire offered me a contract for 1988, which was put back to '89 as I was picked on the England tour for West Indies.

I had expected to build on my first-class debut and make an impact in the 1987 Shell Shield domestic tournament. We had a pre-tournament camp and it was clear that competition for places amongst the fast bowlers was going to be fierce. There was Tony Merrick, who enjoyed some county success at Warwickshire and later Kent, George Ferris and Winston Benjamin, who both played for Leicestershire, and West Indies Test player Eldine Baptiste – and me. I said to myself they are the four senior players so I will probably be in the thirteen but won't start. Anyone who watched the camp actually had me in the XI because I bowled really well. Word on the street was 'Ambrose and who will take the new ball?' I was happy to settle for being the reserve bowler in the thirteen, though. But to the amazement of the whole of Antigua I wasn't in the thirteen, but, what was worse, I wasn't even one of the four reserves. So effectively the selectors were saying I wasn't in their seventeen! To this day I don't know why I was overlooked. It couldn't have been through lack of performing because everyone told me I was the best bowler on show. I was disappointed and puzzled, but it didn't bother me too much. I just went back to work at the garage, before leaving for some more English league cricket.

Winston Benjamin commented: 'Competition in that Leeward Islands team was fierce. We all wanted to fight for a place in the team and once we were in the side we all wanted the ball. I know for a fact that rivalry helped prepare Curtly for when he became a part of the West Indies side. If Malcolm [Marshall] bowled his eight overs for ten runs, the next man wanted to go for nine runs. It used to be quite a battle to be tight or the man who got the job done.'

The start of the 1988 West Indies season was less political – initially – as this time there was no Eldine Baptiste or Winston Benjamin; they were on West Indies duty in India. So I made the team along with Ferris and Merrick. But just when I thought my career was finally taking off, I received an almighty jolt in the shape of more politics. We began our first-class season, which was then called the Red Stripe Cup, away at Guaracara Park against Trinidad & Tobago. They had a good team with a young Brian Lara and Ian Bishop, West Indies fast bowler Tony Gray and veteran batsman Larry Gomes, as their captain. This game was supposed to be my big breakthrough opportunity with Baptiste and Winston Benjamin away. But it did not exactly go to plan. I will never forget this match as the Trinidadian umpire

Clyde Cumberbatch called me for throwing. It was just one delivery, during the second innings of the match. There was talk that a Trinidad player spoke to the umpires about my action and said it was suspect. This spread around the ground so people in the stands started shouting, 'Umpire, watch that guy', 'Umpire, you gotta watch his action, y'know!' It was bizarre because after I bowled the ball deep into my spell, on hearing the no-ball call, I turned to the umpire and inquired, 'How far over?', so I could make the adjustment. I believed it must have been a front-foot infringement. He said, 'It wasn't me', and gestured towards square leg. So I thought maybe there were three men behind square, but there were two. It wasn't a high beamer either, it was a legitimate ball. So we were all puzzled. Ralston Otto – who was a cousin of mine – asked Umpire Cumberbatch why he'd called 'no-ball' but he did not answer the question. To this day I still have not heard an explanation. But we all knew it was for throwing because it couldn't have been for anything else. We thought if an umpire cannot explain why he's called a no-ball then we can't carry on in this way. So we started to walk off the field, until our manager persuaded us to stay on and finish the game.

Ian Bishop, now a respected media analyst, commented: 'I don't think there were politics at play, I just think the umpire made a huge mistake; he got it wrong. But it was not a nice thing for Curtly to have to go through.'

We lost by two wickets as well so it was a disaster of a match for us, but especially me. I knew my action was clean and I never took it personally. I don't believe Ian Bishop or Tony Gray had anything to do with it. Bish is a good friend of mine, though he wasn't then. He would have been too young at the time to have known what was going on. I dismissed it as one of those peculiar things, though I lost respect for Cumberbatch, who was an experienced umpire. In fact, when I went to Trinidad to play Pakistan in a one-day international a couple of months later he was the umpire and he greeted me with a 'Hi, how are you?' I reciprocated and never mentioned the incident because it was clear he'd blundered. But I did lose a lot of respect for him after that. If you're going to call someone for throwing you have to explain yourself.

I played the next match against the Windward Islands and took just three wickets. Somehow, despite my difficult couple of weeks, I managed to keep my place for the third match against Jamaica in St Kitts, even though Eldine and Winston came back. To my surprise they dropped Ferris and Merrick. But I repaid their faith with nine for 92 in the match. Fortunately, whenever I have been faced with adversity in my career I have responded very aggressively and positively. Pride drives me on more than anything and I knew the pressure was on to deliver in this game. From here, it was up, up, up. I followed that match with twelve wickets against Guyana in Antigua. We tore them to pieces.

I added another five wickets in a win against a strong Barbados team at the Kensington Oval. That match really meant a lot as, without wishing to sound insular, I grew up listening to cricket blaring out on my mother's radio and all I ever heard from her or the commentators was how great the Barbados players were, such as Wes Hall, Garfield Sobers, the three Ws, Conrad Hunte and then in more recent times Gordon Greenidge, Desmond Haynes, Malcolm Marshall and Joel Garner. Barbados had a rich legacy and they were so greatly respected throughout the region that they became the team everyone wanted to beat and I was no different. I guess it would be like how so many teams in English football raise their game against the once mighty Manchester United or Liverpool in their heyday. I came from a region that didn't even play as Leeward Islands initially but as the Combined Islands, so we were the little brother that Barbados would normally expect to beat heavily. But as soon as I played for the Leeward Islands, victory over Barbados was as important to me as anything. I had it in my head that they were such great cricketers that I wanted to play against Barbados and beat up on them to show that we are as good as they are. So that win in '88 was special and very satisfying; it was like a mini Test match. Richie Richardson scored 176 while opening the batting against Marshall and Garner and the cricket was incredible. They knew he liked to hook so they tested him often with the short ball – and Richie, like Viv then, never wore a helmet – but he came back at them with some serious hook shots, pull shots and cuts. The intensity of our domestic cricket in those days had a knock-on effect into the West Indies team, and vice versa. This is one area I wish I could say was still the case nowadays. There was no mercy as far too much pride and so many bragging rights were at stake. I even bowled bouncers at Joel Garner and Malcolm Marshall, which stirred the Barbados crowd. They were howling, loving every minute of it. You could sense their fears on my behalf, 'Boy, who's this rookie thinking he can bowl bouncers at Garner and Marshall and get away with it? He's gonna get it now!' That was just my competitive spirit. I actually had Garner caught by Viv at slip off a bouncer though he claimed it hit him on his shoulder. It was a mini battle between 'Big Bird' and 'Little Bird' – as I got called for a while when I first came on the scene. I didn't like that comparison as I wasn't exactly small and we were quite different, but that nickname didn't stick for very long. And when I bounced Marshall he indicated to me that I should expect some of the same when it was my turn to bat. Marshall didn't bowl to me in the event but I did have to sway from a few Garner short balls. It was serious business.

I finished the domestic season with a record-breaking thirty-five wickets, surpassing Winston Davis's thirty-three. It was also the first time that Viv Richards had seen me in full flow and I think he earmarked me then for a West Indies debut, although I didn't know that at the time.

Inside the Greatest Cricket Team

'Our strength, apart from having great players, was a supreme confidence that we couldn't be beaten. We lost games along the way but we prided ourselves on being the best we could be every day. We didn't need a coach to tell us what we had to do – we knew ourselves'

I received a call, indirectly, saying I had been selected for the West Indies team to play Pakistan in the first one-day international in March 1988. A lot of Antiguans were overjoyed yet not really surprised because I had broken the wicket-taking record in domestic cricket. Me? I never thought about it. Whatever happened was fine by me. If I didn't get the call I would have just carried on playing basketball. Actually, the night before I was due to fly to Jamaica for my international debut I was on the basketball court with Swetes, playing a league game. My cricket mentor was – and still is to this day – the former Somerset player and Leeward Islands manager Hugh Gore (or 'Manage' to most of us) and he was livid with my casual attitude. A lot of people questioned why I was playing and told me I could get injured. It seemed my West Indies call-up meant more to everyone else than it did to me. So after all their words of caution I thought, 'Maybe they're right, I should stop.' So I left the game at half-time and watched from the bench. At this stage, as I've said, I honestly believed I could have played basketball at the highest level, the NBA in the States. But that didn't materialise and people close to me continually encouraged me to stick at the cricket. It took me two years as a West Indies player before I started to focus properly on cricket. All the villagers in Swetes kept telling me to knuckle down to the cricket and by 1990 I thought, 'They can't all be wrong, I will give it my all from now on.'

My arrival in the West Indies dressing room, which was stuffed with all-time great players, was not at all intimidating because I had played against all the guys in the regional tournament prior to my selection. It was very easy to walk into that team and feel comfortable, though the fact I already knew Viv Richards, Richie Richardson and Winston Benjamin helped, no doubt. I didn't personally know guys like Gordon Greenidge and Desmond Haynes but it was still a smooth transition for me. I stayed closer to the Leeward guys but because I am a reserved person I was able to sit back and observe the way the team functioned. I'm highly competitive on the field but in the dressing room I'm a bit of a joker. People might be surprised by that because of my serious, on-field manner. Once I've crossed the white line I have my game face on. Away from the ground I'm totally different; I don't want to hear about cricket. The team was full of different personalities. Having got to know the guys I quickly realised Desmond Haynes was similar to me and liked to talk a lot of foolishness, too. So we hit it off. It didn't take me long to feel a part of the team.

Malcolm Marshall was universally recognised as the King of the Pack, amongst the fast bowlers, that is. We were not competitive with one another, we were like a group. We had all heard about the four-pronged attack and knew that it was Malcolm and three others. Courtney was steadily establishing himself, though we did not become the best of friends until 1990. Patrick Patterson was a good bloke, didn't really talk a lot but was a hard worker. He was a ferociously quick fast bowler and only inconsistency let him down over the years, which probably saw me leapfrog him pretty quickly in terms of seniority. I think Viv saw me as a guy who was pretty consistent and got the job done so I went ahead of him. But Patto played his part in some fine wins for West Indies. Winston Benjamin was of course my closest buddy, given our background as school friends. I stuck pretty close to Winston for those first few months in the team as, though I knew others like Viv and Richie, we weren't really friends at that stage.

Malcolm Marshall was someone I learned a lot from in those early years in international cricket, but, if I am brutally honest, we didn't hit it off at first and it probably took us two years before we did. There were a few things that happened that gave me the impression I would have to work real hard to win Marshall's respect. I remember clearly one such instance when a few reporters asked Malcolm on the 1988 tour of England about me. Their question was something along the lines of 'Curtly Ambrose is bowling well – he looks a serious talent for the future?' Marshall replied with the briefest of acknowledgements about my potential, saying I was up and coming, but instead started talking up Ian Bishop and how he was going to be West Indies' new terror in world cricket. Bishop had not played a Test match at that point. I felt it was very dismissive of Marshall not to say anything complimentary about me and to praise Bishop instead. I didn't have a problem with the comments about Ian Bishop because he certainly was destined for greatness but I thought he could have said something about me, too. I was disappointed and that stuck in my mind for a while. It felt like he didn't think I was going to be much good for the West Indies.

There were other times when I felt disrespected by Marshall. I was having a tough period in the second Test at Lord's on that '88 tour and after I was hit for four by Allan Lamb, Marshall complained in an aggressive way: 'Joel Garner never got driven like that!' Joel and I were both six foot eight and bowled a lot of yorkers so we were often compared. This was only my fifth Test match, I had not been playing Test cricket for even six months, and I had expected the leader of our attack – the most experienced bowler, the best bowler in the world as he was then – to come over to me and show some support and lend a few words of encouragement. But instead I was slated for not being as good as Joel. I did not expect that from him and I took it rather personally and felt he could have given me a few pointers as I was still a rookie learning my trade, but that never happened. I thought he was down on me (even though I took twenty-two wickets in that five-Test series in England and then added another twenty-six in Australia a few months later – more than anyone else).

I sat in my hotel room later that night and began to reflect on what Marshall had said and came to the conclusion that, although he probably thought I was no good, I was going to show him he was wrong; I always wanted to be the best I could be at whatever I did. Like many other times in my career, when someone has doubted me I take it as a challenge to prove them wrong. It is the way I have always lived my life. It was not until 1990 that we became closer and that was probably because of my eight for 45 against England at Barbados that finally convinced him that I had what it takes to make it. Once I had earned his respect, we started to talk about cricket much more and I always enjoyed listening to him talk about fast bowling. His advice definitely helped me to develop quicker. We all know about Malcolm Marshall, the great bowler, but his cricket brain was equally impressive. Even when I was a senior bowler and he was coach of the West Indies team, I picked his brains because he had so much knowledge of our art. I hugely respected Malcolm.

> Courtney Walsh said of his early impressions of Curtly: 'I thought, apart from being someone who was tall and skinny like myself, he had some potential. Viv had told me before I met him that he had seen someone from Swetes Village in the nets who had a lot of talent so it wasn't really a surprise when Curtly came through because Viv has a very good eye for talent. Curtly fitted straight in once he joined the team.'

Carl Hooper was very quiet, but what a talent. He made batting look so easy. I played with Carl for years and never saw him struggle. I always admired him for his talent but he never fulfilled his potential and should have scored a lot more runs. His ability was never in question but I don't think he had the burning desire like a Brian Lara. Many people will consider this comment strange but Carl Hooper had more talent than Brian Lara. Carl was supremely talented and made batting look easier than Brian. But Brian knew that talent alone would not take him to the highest level and he matched that with determination and drive, which was where Carl fell down. Shivnarine Chanderpaul is not half as talented as either of those two but his determination drove him to great heights. If Hooper had had the determination of either of those guys I can only imagine what he might have achieved. As I became more established in the team, I came down hard on Carl many times and spoke very aggressively to him with some choice words, some strong language, and I let him know that he was too talented a player not to be scoring more runs. I told him for his own good. I did the same with Brian Lara and many others in the team from time to time. That's how I am. Once I step over the rope I take my cricket very seriously and I expect the same commitment from my team-mates. That was how we remained great; we policed ourselves in terms of standards and competitiveness. We didn't need a coach or manager to tell us where we were going wrong. When I came into the West Indies team we were the best in the world for seven years. Our strength, apart from having great players, was a supreme confidence that we couldn't be beaten. Of course we lost games along the way but we prided ourselves on being the best we could be every single day. I never played with him, but I think that mentality stemmed from the Clive Lloyd era. I heard he was like a father figure and when Viv became captain he continued those high standards.

We approached our training with complete professionalism and high intensity. People ask me all the time 'Did you go easy on your own batsmen in the nets?' The answer: absolutely not! That was one of the reasons why these guys were so good because they honed their techniques against us in the nets and, conversely, we were bowling to great batsmen. It was serious business. There was never a time when we just went through the motions because it was nets. We never did that. We ran in and bowled hard at them and the batsmen had to bat properly. We as bowlers decided this was how it should be; we were going to bowl seriously at our batsmen in the nets so when they went into the middle they would face bowlers not as good as us and score big runs. That was our thinking. The batsmen needed to be sharp because we were all bowling around ninety miles per hour and we bowled bouncers like we would in a game. It was all for a purpose. We bowlers were working on our game and it was up to the batsmen to work on theirs. The guy I enjoyed bowling to most was Desmond Haynes because he enjoyed the competition and, for us, it was Barbados against Antigua. If I bowled him a half-volley and he smacked it down the ground he would say, 'That's four to Desmond Haynes and Barbados are on their way.' But if I nicked his edge I would say, 'Barbados in trouble, two down with just fifteen on the board.' We always had good banter. Jeffrey Dujon liked a bit of fun, too – and was also a good batsman and very good keeper. The guy I didn't much like bowling to was Sir Viv because he hated batting in the nets. He wasn't the Viv we knew in the nets. He felt trapped and enclosed so once he came into nets I looked to bowl at someone else. Gordon Greenidge was different; very quiet, never said much, did his practice and left.

Greenidge recalled those net sessions with some trepidation. 'Net practice was always a tense situation because those guys gave no quarter. You really had to be on your best behaviour during practice. The batters that liked to chatter and got under the skin of the fast bowlers seemed to bring another yard and a half out of them – so I kept quiet! But it was also a good situation as it primed you for whatever you were going to receive out in the middle from the opposition.'

My debut in the first one-day international in Jamaica was initially a tense affair. The local boy, Patrick Patterson, bowled the first over and the whole of Sabina Park was right behind him chanting, 'Rambo, Rambo', though I don't know why they called him that. And when Viv turned to me before the second over and said, 'Big Fella, it's your turn', I was so nervous. Incidentally, although Viv called me Big Fella, to most of the guys I was Ambi – though Winston called me 'Long-brose'. Even though I was full of confidence with my bowling, the whole occasion of that debut got to me. I marked my run-up and once I started running in I couldn't feel anything under my feet. It felt like I was floating in the air. I wasn't thinking about where I was putting the ball, I just wanted to get it over with. Pakistan opener Ramiz Raja took two runs off each of my first two deliveries and then my natural competitive streak kicked in. I said to myself, 'Come on, man, you can't be having this.' I hated giving runs away. Third ball Ramiz inside-edged on to his stumps and Sabina Park was in uproar. The nerves disappeared suddenly and I followed up with another three wickets including Javed Miandad and Imran Khan to cap my debut with figures of four for 39.

The second ODI was at the ARG, though Mum didn't come as she preferred to watch the television with the sound down and listen to the commentary on the radio. But my brother Danny flew in from New Jersey. Incidentally, somewhere around this time Mum started a tradition that the whole world seemingly became aware of. She rang a bell outside the family home in Swetes every time I took a wicket for the West Indies. I never even knew this until a reporter asked me about it. Just a word on that bell; it was gifted to her by Anesta in 1982. My sister was studying in Kingston, Jamaica, and working with children with hearing difficulties hence the reason she had a bell on her. Mum still has that bell at home.

Back to the ARG, Gordon was captain in Viv's absence and their styles were quite different. Gordon was quiet whereas Viv was very aggressive. Gordon hardly raised his voice but he could be aggressive when he wanted. Once he reached a point where he couldn't take any more he would let you have it. But he could absorb a lot. Unlike me, who could burn on a short fuse. I added four for 35 in that game before another two wickets in the third ODI. I was then rested for the Test series.

Any nerves I had back in Jamaica had long since disappeared and I started to settle in as part of the team. We lost the first Test in Guyana badly by nine wickets. It was a difficult first match for me, as I finished their first innings with figures of two for 108 from twenty-eight overs. It was hard on my pride to take, going for more than a hundred runs. I promised myself that day in Georgetown that I would never go for more than a hundred runs again in a Test innings, unless I bowled more than thirty-five overs. Thankfully I kept my promise for the next ninety-seven Test matches and never did go over the hundred mark again!

Pakistan played better than us but we weren't despondent and still felt we would come back. It was tough, though, as Pakistan had a great team. On reflection, they played the better cricket through that series and they had us on the ropes a lot but our character pulled us through to a 1-1 series draw. The main difference was their inspirational skipper and fast bowling great Imran Khan and their master batsman Javed Miandad, who scored centuries in the first two Tests. That was the first time I saw Miandad at length and I felt he was a dogged kind of player. He frustrated me – then and all through the years I played against him. Some batsmen tried to play shots against me and I didn't mind that as it gave me a bit of a challenge. But Miandad, in Test cricket, would try to bat all day by clipping a single here and dab for two there. He would turn good balls into ones and twos and it frustrated me greatly. He was a class player. He would raise his bat for a fifty and you'd try and figure out where the hell did those runs come from. I hated bowling at him because he didn't give you a chance. Javed was totally different in one-day cricket, though, and could be dangerous.

The second Test was drawn before a nail-biter in Barbados, where we never used to lose. We had to win to keep our unbeaten series record alive that had spanned eight years. Strangely enough, we had to rely on an unlikely match-winner in Winston Benjamin (40 not out) and Jeff Dujon (29 not out) also, as they played great knocks, especially Winston, who wasn't known for his batting. They added 61 for the ninth wicket. After the win, Viv became emotional in the dressing room and cried a bit. You could see the tears streaming down his face. That was the first and only time I have seen Viv cry. He was just so proud that his team pulled through in such a tight situation. Viv loved to see the guys fight and that emotion came from his pride at the battling qualities we demonstrated, especially from a youngster like Winston.

Hello, England

*'We felt that while England were messing around with so
many captains and all those players they never had a chance
of beating us. We knew they were in disarray and never had
a hope of winning a game'*

My Test match baptism had been a very tough one against
Pakistan and, if the selectors had had their way, I might never
have made the 1988 tour to England. I only took seven wickets
in three games at fifty-two apiece against Pakistan. And having
come off the one-day series with ten wickets in three matches
there was talk that I was more suited for one-day cricket. People
were judging me straight away. Viv told me he had to convince
the selectors that I had greatness just for them to pick me for the
England tour. And Viv is a man who can spot talent. It was a nice
confidence boost to hear someone like Viv Richards say that to
me but it also told me there was a serious question mark over
my place, so I still had to win a lot of people over. Fortunately I
didn't disappoint Viv or my team and didn't look back from this

tour onwards. Those couple of seasons playing league cricket in 1986 and 1987 gave me useful exposure to English conditions so the cold and rain was not so much of a culture shock when I returned with the West Indies.

One of the things on my mind when we started this tour was winning the series 5-0. I thought because West Indies had won 5-0 on their last tour to England in '84 and then 5-0 in the Caribbean in '86, it would be nice to be a part of another 5-0 team. In the lead-up games against the counties we came up against the new golden boy of English cricket, the Zimbabwean Graeme Hick. He was serving his residency qualification period to play for England and he also served us early notice of his promise by scoring 172. I thought it was a good knock because of the standard of our bowling attack. There was myself, Bishop, Walsh and Patterson, so it's not like we put out an inferior attack. It was a very strong bowling line-up and Hick played extremely well to get those runs because we didn't give them away – he had to earn them. It was a great innings, actually. I made a mental note of that young man and placed it to the back of my memory bank until our next meeting. I thought 'next time we meet, I will be ready for you, Mr Hick'.

The first Test at Trent Bridge was drawn – only because of rain. I remember how the English tabloids came out saying, 'England are finally ready to bash the West Indies after coming off two 5-0 whitewashes'. They felt England would match West Indies but ended up getting beat 4-0. Marshall had a great series with thirty-five wickets; they just couldn't negotiate him – he could do no wrong. I ended up with twenty-two so I was pleased with my effort. They dropped Patrick Patterson after the first two Tests and brought in Winston Benjamin and I then started taking the new ball with Marshall, ahead of Courtney Walsh even though he was a senior player to me. Graham Gooch played well in that first Test with his hundred (146); he was a stubborn cricketer, not very attractive to watch but he got the job done. I scored 43 and actually used to bat much better in the first half of my career than the second half, because my workload as a bowler became a lot heavier later on as the likes of Marshall, Bishop and Patterson left the scene. There was more responsibility on me as a bowler and that had an impact on my batting, which fell away quite badly.

The talk about Lord's, where we won the second Test, had no effect on me. It was just another game. The Lord's hype came years later for me, when I was more into my cricket. I never did get on to that honours board, but I did take four wickets in an innings on three occasions. Marshall, though, took ten in this game and was at the peak of his powers. At Manchester, Maco was dominant again with seven for 22 in the second innings – he was unplayable. I'll never forget that day as it was one of the best displays of fast bowling I've ever seen. The ball was going all over the place – he made that ball talk, though I did not have any sympathy for England. We were not complacent and didn't want to give England a sniff. I was man of the match at Leeds for my seven wickets. Here, England brought in Chris Cowdrey as their third captain of the series (there were to be four, officially) and we thought it was ridiculous that they should bring in a guy because he was supposedly a good leader of his county side, Kent in his case. He lasted one game! It was pure madness. I had never seen it before and never saw it again. England kept changing every game and you can't win Test matches like that. You need to stay together. The series was a disaster for them: four captains and twenty-three players. But we never spoke much of England's problems. We just felt that while they were messing around with so many captains and all those players they never had a chance of beating us. We knew they were in disarray and never had a hope of winning a game.

This series was the first time I had any contact with Allan Lamb, who was to be my new captain at Northamptonshire the following year. Therefore, I knew my reputation was at stake during that series. There was no way I was going to give Lamby the chance to rib me in the dressing room the following season about the way he had got the better of me so I peppered him. He scored a good hundred at Lord's but I got him in both innings at Old Trafford and then at Headingley, where I really went after him while he was struggling with a sore hamstring. We were not team-mates then so I wasn't going to go easy on him. I knew he had a good record against West Indies so I wanted to make things a little more uncomfortable for him. I used to take the same attitude into regional games against the likes of Greenidge and Haynes as I didn't want them to have any bragging rights over me in the West Indies dressing room.

> Ian Edwards, one of Curtly's trusted long-time friends, said: 'Curtly was well aware of what the likes of Andy Roberts had achieved before him. So when he got into the West Indies team, following Roberts and also Holding and Garner, he didn't want to be the weak link to break the chain. That was out of pride. The honour of representing the West Indies energised him.'

We sealed a comprehensive series win at The Oval. We were satisfied with 4-0 and were not in any way frustrated. Although we all wanted it to be 5-0, there's always the chance of bad weather in England so 4-0 was a good result. I was pleased for us to win the series so convincingly and that I managed to take those twenty-two wickets. But the thing that gave me more personal satisfaction was that my performances silenced those people who claimed that I was 'just a one-day bowler' before the tour squad was announced. I certainly hadn't yet arrived as a Test cricketer but those twenty-two wickets were very pleasing as my critics had to eat their words. I felt very comfortable with life off the pitch as well though I never really got up to too much when I toured. I don't drink and I'm not one of those guys who stay out late at bars or anything like that. Typically for me, if we batted all day and I had some energy I might go out for dinner with Winston.

Romantically, my life was about to change for the long term when I met my wife-to-be, Bridget. I had known her before I played Test cricket, as we used to see each other around. She was actually a very good netball player and that was how I saw her first. I was smitten by her looks straight away and suddenly found myself paying more attention to netball. When I found out that she was from All Saints Village, I asked Winston about her because he is from there also and I assumed he must know her. He told me she was his cousin; that made it easier for me to arrange an introduction. We started going out and became serious once I returned from England in '88. I left for Australia soon after we met so it was an early test of our relationship, but we got used to it. We kept in contact throughout the

Australia tour, though Bridget was curious as to whether we would still be together by the time I returned and was concerned that a three-month tour like this would end our relationship. This was at a time when I was slowly becoming a superstar and, with being so early in our relationship, she was feeling insecure. I assured her she didn't need to feel that way as I was smitten. Such is the life of a touring cricketer! We were married in 2001, after I finished playing cricket, because there never seemed to be enough time to get married while I was playing, though she would spend four months in England with me every time I played county cricket, which made things easier on us. She had always loved cricket and knew a lot about the sport before we met. Bridget would actually remind me of things I had done in games.

When I met Bridget she had a two-year-old girl Latoya, who I helped raise as if she was my own. She now lives in Vancouver, working as a criminologist, and has a four-year-old daughter. We had our first daughter, Tanya, in 1990. She was born at the Northampton General Hospital, while I was in England playing county cricket. Tanya is now studying to be a nurse in New Jersey, after changing her mind about her initial career choice. We had Chloe in 1998, born in New Jersey before I was able to get there in time. I had told WICB president Wes Hall that I would not be available for the one-day series against England because I planned on being with Bridget for the birth of my second child. But I got the call in Antigua that Chloe had arrived early, so I called Wes Hall back up and said, 'Change of plan, I'm available.' I always say to Chloe she was in a hurry to enter this world.

Bridget and I wanted a boy next. We thought we must be due a son, but Beyoncé came in 2002, also born in New Jersey. I named our first two girls but Tanya insisted her second sister be named after her favourite pop star from the band Destiny's Child. We were happy to go along with it. We also adopted Annie after she had lived with us from the age of nine – she is now twenty-one. She is half-Indian and her real name is Shushanna but we've always called her Annie. She and Bridget had developed a very close loving mother–daughter relationship while Bridget worked at her school as a physical education teacher. Annie's mother was on hard times and struggling financially, as she had three other children to care for as well. It was felt that it would be the best outcome for Annie and her mother if we adopted her. Initially I needed some convincing that it was a good idea given we already had three girls, but after a while I thought it was the logical thing to do as she had lived with us for years anyway. She's a wonderful, respectful girl and I love her like she's my own. She calls me Daddy and I'm glad she's part of our family.

Chloe isn't sure what she wants to do yet but will likely be a model or a film star as she's more for the glamorous side of life and very into fashion. Tanya, Beyoncé and Annie are more down to earth. I love my girls dearly, even if I didn't get the son I always hoped for! If we had continued trying for a boy I might have ended up with a cricket team – of girls.

Australia, I'm Coming for You

'I cleaned up Border for a duck in his 100th Test. I softened him up with a few short ones and then bowled him out, which is what bouncers are all about for me'

My 'love affair' with Australia began on this tour, my first trip Down Under. I say that because I always had success there and because it was the first time I started to feel that I'd arrived in Test cricket. We won the series 3-1 and I took twenty-six wickets and felt like I was a serious threat against some top players – and a much better, more settled team than we had faced in England. It was a powerful side with Allan Border, David Boon, Geoff Marsh, Steve Waugh, Craig McDermott and others. For me, everything felt right as it was my kind of climate and the pitches had more pace in them generally. The odds were stacked against us, though. We never had many supporters out there as it's a long way to travel and very expensive for West Indian fans. So we didn't have too many people behind us. It felt like a group of guys taking on the whole of Australia so the series win from that perspective was very satisfying. In Melbourne it was 100,000 against eleven. It was different in England because there are a lot of West Indians living there, but that's not the case in Australia. Saying that, I liked the way the Australian players and their public appreciated our cricket, even when we were beating their boys, sometimes quite badly. They give you plenty of stick during the matches, but if you do well they also respect you and say 'well played'. They had a strong, competitive team in this series, as usual, and it was clear to me that Allan Border was moulding a good side, having already won the World Cup a year prior. They had the players and I was not surprised they eventually toppled us and became number one. But at this stage, we were still the kings and were determined not to let our title slip.

We won the first Test in three and a half days and I managed to dismiss the great Allan Border in both innings, which was a good confidence boost. Steve Waugh played well for his 90 but contrary to popular opinion I wouldn't say this was the start of our rivalry. Although he was a bit of a thorn in our flesh in that series, our rivalry probably began a little later in our careers. At this stage he wasn't a great player, but useful and certainly gritty. He was actually quite effective with the ball in those days. I had David Boon as a better batsman then. We went 2-0 up in Perth despite a heroic bowling effort from Merv Hughes, who took thirteen wickets in the match. Merv bowled real well, especially considering Geoff Lawson was injured for the second innings. He had a reputation for being a joker with that silly moustache and not looking anything like an athlete, but he was a competitor and a better bowler than most people gave him credit for. As for Lawson, I put him in hospital after he missed a bouncer that unfortunately fractured his jaw. He had a helmet on but I don't think he was wearing a faceguard. The ball went on to the stumps and knocked a bail off and he should have been out but we were more concerned about his safety. We didn't realise it at the time so he was given 'retired hurt'. I went to see him in hospital later that day, along with our manager, Clive Lloyd, and a few of the boys. I was genuinely concerned about his wellbeing. There is a misconception that we West Indian fast bowlers are happy to knock batsmen out rather than get them out but that's not true. I want to get batsmen out first and foremost but if you are being stubborn I have to find ways and means within the laws of the game to get you out, so I try things, and bouncers are part of cricket, part of a fast bowler's tool kit. So if I have to bowl a few bouncers to unsettle you – that will hopefully give me a better chance to get you out. But it's not just us who dish it out; our guys have been hurt also. It's part of the game.

We retained the Frank Worrell Trophy in Melbourne with a big win. I was man of the match for my six wickets and first innings 44, which was a crucial knock in the circumstances. I cleaned up Border for a duck in his 100th Test. I softened him up with a few short ones and then bowled him out, which is what bouncers are all about. They unsettle a batsman before following up with a wicket-taking delivery. The Australian public weren't too happy. 'Who is this Curtly Ambrose to bowl this way to the great Allan Border?' They gave me some stick and didn't like it. To me, it was evidence of Malcolm Marshall's influence rubbing off as he was always talking to us younger guys about setting batsmen up. He made us think hard about our bowling and talked us through situations. I thrive on competition and the better the batsman meant the better I had to be so that is why I always relished the battle against the best players rather than cowering at what they might do to me. If I can get great players like Allan Border, Graham Gooch, Javed Miandad out, it means I am doing the right things. I didn't say much in team meetings at that stage because I didn't know how to get Allan Border out or the other guys so I would listen hard to people like Viv and I would remember certain things that would be useful. For instance, I remember the guys saying Border was not the greatest of hookers – not that he couldn't play it but he wasn't so strong there. Driving and cutting were his strengths so I'd try to eliminate the drives and cuts and try to tuck him up a bit more. I had him in the first Test caught by Desmond Haynes while fending off a bouncer so it was a tactic that worked for me against him.

One final word on that MCG Test: Patrick Patterson took nine wickets in the match, including five for 39 in the second innings. He was seriously upset by the hard time that he and other tail-enders in our team had received from the Aussie fielders, as we frustrated them. There was a bit of name-calling like 'who's this rabbit?' and such like. Well, after play a reporter came to Viv and said that one of our players was causing a disturbance in the Australian dressing room. It so happened that Patto was over there telling the Aussie players in his Jamaican patois, 'We will see who the rabbits are tomorrow.' Viv brought him back over before he went any further. We all thought, 'Boy, Patto is upset – it could be trouble for the Australians tomorrow.' He went out there and bowled ferociously quick and blew Australia to pieces. I played with him from 1988 to 1992 and that was the quickest I ever saw him bowl. I can tell you that none of the Australians fancied him in that mood.

The fact we were 3-0 up after three Tests should not give the impression that this Australia team was soft because they were not. It had more to do with that West Indies team still being at the peak of its powers. Greenidge, Haynes, Richardson, Richards, Hooper, Logie, Dujon, Marshall, Ambrose, Walsh and Patterson – that was a seriously strong unit and few teams in history could have lived with us.

You would not have thought that, though, if you saw our performance in the next Test at Sydney. Part-time spinner Allan Border took eleven wickets in the match and they beat us comfortably. The manner of our defeat (we lost eighteen wickets to spin in the Test) started all those old clichés again that the West Indies were vulnerable to spin. Those comments are nonsense. We might come up against a spinner in a five-Test series and if he has one good match all of a sudden we can't play spin, totally forgetting the four not so good matches that spinner might have had. The Indian leg-spinner Narendra Hirwani took sixteen wickets against West Indies in one match but what did he do against West Indies after that? Nothing! But we still hear this talk. People are clutching at straws. The great Shane Warne – and he *was* great – bowled us out in one match at Melbourne in '92, but how often did he destroy West Indies? Seldom: he averaged thirty against us overall so what does that tell you? It tells me that when you get a great team, too many people are scratching around looking for weaknesses that aren't there. If Warne or these guys keep bowling West Indies out almost every game then I might agree there is something in this theory but I don't – it's complete crap. Viv Richards, Desmond Haynes, Brian Lara – these were great players of spin.

What cost us more at Sydney was that our spinner didn't turn up. Patrick Patterson rattled the Australians with his pace at the MCG, took nine wickets, yet was still dropped for Sydney as it was felt, quite rightly you have to say having seen the Australian wicket-takers, we needed a front-line spinner. So Roger Harper came in for Patto but didn't take a wicket in thirty-seven overs. Viv was extremely mad that a part-time spinner like Border could take eleven and our front-line spinner didn't take one. Harps would admit himself he had a really poor game, but we didn't hold it against him because he didn't mean to bowl badly. He only played one more Test for the West Indies again after this match, four years later in Sri Lanka. It was a tough decision to leave out Patto for the spinner but it didn't work out for us. We were also disappointed with that defeat because we wanted to close out the series 5-0. We had a mentality that when our opponents are down, you keep them down. The fifth Test was drawn on a flat one but we were happy to win the series. Socially it was a very uneventful tour for me because, not being a drinker or a night owl, I tended mostly to stay around the team hotel.

From the euphoria of a breakthrough series in Australia I was brought straight back down to earth in our next series against India in the Caribbean. It was one of those series where nothing much went right for me. I didn't go for many runs but finished with just five wickets in four Tests, which didn't compare very well with the other guys: Marshall 19 wickets in three Tests, Walsh 18 in four and Bishop 16 in four. The positives, apart from a convincing 3-0 series win, were, one, that I wasn't dropped, and, two, that the likes of Viv and the guys were still behind me and encouraging me. But just when I thought it was a minor blip in my career that I would soon overcome, the great Michael Holding came out with a comment about me that took me by surprise. It wasn't too derogatory but he said in a newspaper – to use his Jamaican language – 'Strong abroad and weak ah yard.' Or in other words, bowls well abroad, but not so good at home. I took it as motivation – and to be fair to Michael there was some truth to it as I had taken twelve wickets in seven games at home, which was not good enough. Unfortunately I had to wait almost a year to make my point, with only a one-day tour to India for the rest of the year. But make my point I did.

The King of Kensington

'Robert Bailey was looking for excuses for his failed international career . . . I told him, "That thigh pad wicket – I don't want it. I am one wicket less. I've heard enough about this costing you your England career. It is nonsense!"'

There was a significant turning point in my career prior to the 1990 home series against England. It wasn't long before this time that, even though I was in the West Indies team, I had still hoped to play basketball rather than cricket for a living. But that changed when people I respected in Swetes Village convinced me to give more focus to my cricket and the second reason why I gave up my basketball dream came soon after. It happened when the West Indies selectors left me out of the first Test against England in Jamaica in 1990. Anyone who knows me would tell you that as soon as my ability is called into question that's when I am at my most dangerous. And in this instance the selectors got it badly wrong when they decided – for whatever reason – to leave me out of that team.

It all stemmed from the time I was taken ill during the Leeward Islands' last match of that domestic season, when we won all five first-class games for the clean sweep. It was nothing serious and I soon recovered but still went to see a doctor in Jamaica. I was going to get a second opinion back home in Antigua but the West Indies Cricket Board intervened and said they would take care of me and organised the appointment. At that time an England XI was playing Jamaica and the team for the first Test was set to be announced after that match. But for some reason they named the team *during* the game – before my doctor's appointment – and clearly were not interested in waiting to hear the outcome of my visit to the doctor to see if I was fit to play. There was a lot of speculation as to why I wasn't selected. They would probably have reasoned that I wasn't fit, but how could they say that when they had not even inquired about my doctor's appointment? I say I was dropped, as nobody ever called me to ask about my health, which would be the normal procedure if I had been left out on health grounds. It was the only time I was dropped in my career. I had a poor series against India a year before, which was my previous Test series, but I had bowled well enough since then for the Leeward Islands and West Indies in the Nehru Cup in India. It would not have been so bad if I had been *genuinely* dropped as the attack would have been good without me and I would have said, 'OK, good luck to them.' But the way it was handled left a sour taste and it was another early brush with West Indies Cricket Board politics.

We lost that Test as England beat us for the first time in sixteen years. And here's when things took another twist. They named the same team for the next Test in Guyana and still I was not included. I got over it and went down to the Sugar Factory Ground in Antigua, where I practised for the Combined Parish league team. While I was there my mentor Hugh Gore passed on a message that Malcolm Marshall had an injury and was not going to Guyana so they selected me. I told Hugh I would not go. My take on it was, 'If I wasn't fit enough yesterday, how can I be fit today?' But Hugh convinced me to go and prove them wrong. That was the final source of motivation that I needed to really knuckle down to my cricket and be one of the best around for many years. The Test at Bourda was washed out but they played a one-day match on the scheduled final day instead. I took four for 18 in nine overs: end of mystery – I was fit!

I was on a mission to prove the selectors, the cricket board and whoever else wrong. I knew I could make this cricket thing work for a long time. It was nothing to do with being fitter or training harder as I was naturally a fit person anyway and I always practised hard. It was more about mental focus and this unexpected jolt was what I needed to give me that focus. The one positive aside to the politics is that they never surfaced in the dressing room as long as I was part of it. We were always together and worked to achieve one common goal.

I came back into the team for the third Test in Trinidad. England chased 151 to win and were on course at 120 for five when the rain-hit match was abandoned, for bad light in the end. England should have won that game. The turning point in the match, maybe even in the series, was Ezra Moseley breaking Graham Gooch's hand with a short ball. He had to retire hurt and it changed the whole momentum. Up to that point we were struggling as they were cruising towards victory and a 2-0 series lead. We would either have drawn the series or lost it. The English media said Desmond Haynes, who was captaining in the absence of Viv, was wasting time but there were genuine problems with saturated run-ups. Ezra was bowling because he had a short run-up. I remember having to stop a few times; as a fast bowler you need the ground to be solid. My assessment is that we probably shouldn't have been on for as long as we were. I have encountered it many times in my career where the umpires believe the pitch to be dry so they play but the run-ups are wet. They don't care about the fast bowlers sprinting in on the moisture. I have argued about that for many years. There was also a bit of time-wasting by us, partly because of the soggy ground conditions, but we were not just going to go out there and give the game to England. We were fighting to survive (only 16.5 overs were bowled in one hour and fifty-five minutes). I don't mind admitting, though, we were a bit fortunate to draw this game.

During the Trinidad game the esteemed commentator Tony Cozier, who's from Barbados, was suggesting that I was still unfit and wasn't quite ready for the games. I did not understand his comments because I thought I bowled quite well in the first innings with four for 59 (in 36.2 overs). I felt there was more behind these comments than just an observation on my fitness. I believe it was a campaign to influence the selectors. The great Malcolm Marshall was returning from injury to play at his home ground in Barbados. No argument there; so that meant one of Ambrose, Walsh,

Moseley and Bishop would have to make way for Maco. Walsh and Bishop always seemed likely to play so then it came down to me and Ezra Moseley, who was from Barbados. I could be wrong but I felt that Cozier's comments were designed to lead the selectors towards dropping me and retaining Moseley. I was at a serious crossroads in my career, having just returned from being dropped, and his comments motivated me once more – and I was already fired up from the way the board had treated me before the first Test. So, boy, was I ready to let England have it at the Kensington Oval.

The plot thickened two days before the fourth Test in Barbados when there was a one-day international and myself and Courtney Walsh shared the new ball. Courtney had never taken the new ball before. It was usually two of myself, Ian Bishop, Malcolm Marshall and Patrick Patterson – never Courtney Walsh. So Courtney and I realised pretty quickly this was a trial between the two of us to see who would get the nod for the Test match. Moseley was in along with Marshall and Bishop. The fourth spot was between Ambrose and Walsh. That was the moment when myself and Courtney became close. Until then we were team-mates but we were not close. We had a little talk and I said to him straight up, 'One of us is going to be dropped for the Test match but let's not worry about that. This is the West Indies and we must do our best for the team. If you get the nod ahead of me I wish you all the very best.' And he said the same to me. There was no rivalry from that point and our strong friendship was cemented at that moment. It grew stronger when we were room-mates on the Pakistan tour later in the year. In Barbados we could have thought, 'I will try and outbowl him' but that was never the case. As it happened he took one for 49 and I was wicketless in nine overs but because Courtney had gone at over six runs per over I got the nod for the Test. Those who were obsessed about WICB politics suggested I was selected because the next match was in Antigua and if it had been Jamaica they would have gone with Courtney instead. There is always politics floating around in West Indies cricket and it is no different today.

We were up against it by the time the fourth Test came around. We were 1-0 down with two Test matches left, trying desperately to preserve our proud record of being unbeaten in a Test series for the last ten years. That England team was a good one, quite unlike the more timid sides of the recent past that we had encountered. Curiously, it was without the greats like Ian Botham and David Gower but was still a competitive unit. They were much improved from that disastrous summer of 1988 when they had four captains and about fifty-six players. To have come to the Caribbean two years later and given us such a fight was an impressive achievement. They showed maturity and did not seem as intimidated as they had been in recent times. Winning that first Test in Jamaica was the key and gave them a lot of belief.

I bowled OK in the first innings, picking up a couple of wickets, but I wasn't at my best. Lamby scored a very good hundred while deputising as captain for the injured Gooch. During that innings I really felt like the Barbados crowd turned on me as I was hearing comments like, 'Ambrose, you're bowling crap', or that I shouldn't have been playing. Come the second innings, England were never going to reach their target of 356 and were on the verge of drawing the game, having recovered well from ten for three. It was not your typical fast and bouncy Barbados pitch and was a little up and down. They would certainly have been happy to draw the match as that would have meant they could not lose the series.

Then Viv took the second new ball and threw it to me and said, 'Ambi, do something magical.' Jack Russell was still there, being very stubborn, as usual. He almost took that game away from us. He was a good wicketkeeper and a tough little batter, very gritty. Jack was one of the few people in international cricket who used to irritate me. Why? Just look at him. He wore a hat that he must have got from W.G. Grace, his pads didn't fit right, he always looked untidy, he never looked like an athlete or a sportsperson and when he was batting he was just an irritation. I wanted to get rid of him quickly, to get him out of my sight. But I respected him as a fighter and I know he's a good bloke. There were never any words between us – it was just the way he looked that got to me. I used to think, 'Man, you're not a cricketer, you don't look the part.' I've seen some of his paintings and they are real good; maybe his look was more suited to being a painter. I used to say to Courtney, who played with Russell for many years at Gloucestershire, 'Look at this guy . . .' But Courtney would say, 'I know, he always looks like that but he's a good bloke.' Jack could hang around – but not for long on this occasion. I bowled him with one that kept a little low, hitting the stumps halfway up. That opened them up as Russell and Robin Smith looked as though they were going to close the game out. But from the safety of 166 for five they soon collapsed to 191 all out as I finished with my career-best figures of eight for 45, and ten in the match. There was little in the way of sideways movement and on this pitch I figured batsmen were not going to be caught by the wicketkeeper or in the slip cordon. So my plan was to bowl very straight – wicket to wicket – and hope the odd ball kept low as I would have a great chance of getting them out bowled or leg before, because there was nothing in the pitch. My plan worked beautifully. After the Russell wicket I finished England off with four lbw decisions, trapping Nasser Hussain, David Capel, Phil DeFreitas and Devon Malcolm.

Courtney Walsh, dropped for that game in Barbados, managed to catch some of the action on television and was in awe of Curtly's inspired display: 'It showed the stature of the man, having been left out earlier in that series. He has a never-say-die attitude; always gives 100 per cent. None of us like to be dropped so the way he bounced back showed his character.'

It was the first of the four best spells of my career – and firmly in the top three. The others are my six for 34 against South Africa in Barbados, six for 24 against England in Trinidad and the seven for one (seven for 25 final analysis) in Perth, which ranks fourth because of the match situation. People ask me to explain how I can inflict these devastating, match-winning spells and I believe the simple answer is about having the strength of character to overcome adversity as all these spells came in situations when the team was up against it. Here in Barbados against England it looked as though they were going to hang on for the draw and go into the final Test 1-0 up. I was not having that. Great cricketers fight against the odds and more often than not come out triumphant. When things are going your way, everything comes natural and easy. But when your backs are against the wall and you are down for the count, can you beat the count, get up and win? That is what separates the great cricketers from the average. Myself and Courtney Walsh have worked together in tandem through several of those moments and that has been where our true greatness always shines. It is about having sheer determination that we are not going to lose. I was always confident, believed that I could not lose and I was wholly determined not to lose. It is more than skill. Everybody has the skill to go and bowl or bat. Implementing and executing your skills when all seems lost – that is what makes the difference. I thrive on challenges, negative comments or anything where people doubt my ability. More often than not when I have been faced with those challenges I have come out triumphant.

Team-mate Gordon Greenidge admired Curtly's ability to switch gears when adversity confronted him or his team, like at Kensington when the draw loomed: 'That is where great bowlers step up and deliver; when the chips are down. That was an excellent spell. He bowled with control and pace. I was privileged to have witnessed it not as a spectator but in a front-row seat at third slip. At times I wished I wasn't there because he was bowling with such pace you knew a nick could come fizzing towards you.'

After the match sections of the crowd ran on to the field and embraced me – all of a sudden I was a hero again. These were the same Barbados spectators who were abusing me during England's first innings and didn't think I could bowl. And two days before I shouldn't even have been in the team. I just shrugged and accepted it as the nature of our cricket. West Indian people are the hardest to please. One day you are the greatest, the next you are the worst. I never held a grudge against anyone and just got on with it. I have always been able to accept criticism, whether it is fair or unfair. I used to have conversations with West Indies fans after a day's play and some would say, 'Ambrose, man, you're bowling crap!' I'd just say, 'Can't a man have a bad day?'

One controversy that surfaced in Barbados was the dismissal of my Northamptonshire team-mate Rob Bailey in the second innings, when he was given out caught down the leg side off my bowling. Replays appeared to show that the ball struck his thigh pad. Personally I didn't think it was out at the time. I heard a noise so instinctively I started to go up but pretty quickly I thought, 'I don't think he's hit that' and felt it was probably his thigh pad and so I ceased my appeal right there. I only appeal when I think I've got you out or if I think it's very close; I don't appeal for nonsense. Viv and the guys at the back thought they had him, started the celebration and Lloyd Barker gave him out. Of course I then celebrated because it's a Test wicket. It is not my job to decide what is and is not a wicket. That is for the umpire. Later on when back in the Northants dressing room I heard Rob Bailey say that dismissal ruined his England career and I took offence at it, because that's rubbish. Robert Bailey played in Trinidad – he got a pair so you could say he was fortunate even to be playing in Barbados. OK, he got a bad decision in the second innings but he was out for just 17 in the first innings. He went to Antigua for the fifth Test, so had another chance, and scored 42 and eight. Given those low scores, how could that one bad decision have cost him his career? He was looking for excuses for his failed international career and I was highly annoyed when I heard him say those things. I told him, 'That thigh pad wicket – I don't want it. I am one wicket less. I've heard enough about this costing you your England career. It is nonsense!' I thought it was an unfair statement. I was close to getting physical, too, because I was really angry. None of the other guys said anything and Robert didn't say much either. I said my piece, in an aggressive manner, and moved on. I'm a very straightforward person. If I have something to tell you, I will tell you, without being disrespectful. Once I have said what I want to say, I'm back to normal. If someone holds a grudge, that wouldn't bother me. But if I saw them again and said, 'Hello' and they ignored me, I wouldn't interfere with them again.

On the topic of my Northants mates, I have since heard a few comments that I ignored all of them, after they had 'looked after' me for the previous English summer. Well, all I can say to that is 'Nonsense'. That stuff is not true. Lamby and David Capel were there and we would chat now and again. Wayne Larkins and Rob Bailey were also there. In general I wasn't one for interacting with opponents anyway but it was not intentional or anything to do with me holding on to my 'mystery man' reputation, as some have suggested. I could have a long chat or a laugh with any cricketer in an evening, but once I step over that rope we can forget about the laughs or the drinks I have bought you because it's serious business now. I'm a reserved man anyway and even my team-mates would tell you that, when I'm not joking around, I'd be chilling with some music in the corner of the dressing room, relaxing.

But once we step over that rope, it's business. They want to win, I want to win, there's no time for talk during the game. At the end of the day's play maybe we would then have a little chat about it so there's no truth in those stories. And Viv as a captain never told us who we could and couldn't speak to. His attitude was, 'You're a professional, you're a man, make your own decisions on who to speak to.' Nobody in our team would ever tell another person not to speak to someone. It might have occurred in other teams, but definitely not ours.

We went to Antigua and won by an innings to snatch the series 2-1. Greenidge and Haynes put on almost 300 for the first wicket. We should have scored many more than 446 but it turned out to be enough. England missed Robin Smith in the second innings after he retired hurt with a nasty blow on the hand. He was a good cricketer who I always admired. He relished the contest and if you wanted to do well against a West Indies pace attack of that time you needed a big heart, plenty of fight and the will to succeed. Without those qualities you would not last against us. Smith had those qualities – Allan Lamb and Graham Gooch were the same. We used to cop a lot of flak for the injuries we inflicted but if batsmen do not play the short ball very well then as a fast bowler I will prey on that weakness. And the same tactic can work if a batsman plays the short ball well because a strength can also be a weakness – this is the reason why we went after Smith. It is part of a fast bowler's arsenal. Smith didn't mind hooking so my take was, 'OK, you like to hook. Let's see how good you hook.' I was happy to feed him a few short ones in the hope that he would mistime one. I ended that series with twenty wickets in just three Tests. It was a major turning point in my career. I faced adversity but came through having improved my reputation with some very good performances.

We toured Pakistan before the year was out, for three Tests and three one-day internationals. It was my first trip there and it was a good tour for the team under Desmond Haynes's captaincy, while Viv Richards recovered from surgery. We drew the Test series 1-1 and lost 3-0 in the one-dayers. It was the battle of two great pace attacks with Marshall, Ambrose, Walsh and Bishop lining up against Wasim Akram, Imran Khan and Waqar Younis. Imran Khan was a great leader and a great bowler, while we were impressed with how they all swung the ball at pace. But if I had to choose my favourite from that group I would have to say Akram is my boy for pure variety. He was a great exponent of the art of fast bowling. If the ball is swinging he could make batsmen look stupid. If the ball is not swinging he could use the pitch and still make you look stupid and uncomfortable. The ball didn't have to be swinging for him to be a threat. We should have won that Test series, having lost the first match but then drawn level in Faisalabad. Ian Bishop and myself took five wickets apiece in the first innings in Karachi in the third Test and they were set 346 to win on an uneven pitch. We had them 90 for two after the fourth day but Imran Khan (who batted for 196 balls) and the nightwatchman Masood Anwar (130 balls for 37) held us up; they fought very well. That was Brian Lara's Test debut. Even in those days we could see he was going to be something special, as it proved in future years. That series hurt us as Pakistan had bossed us in the Caribbean two years before when I made my debut.

Therefore we wanted to reassert our dominance over them and show them in their own backyard who the kings of cricket were. But they fought hard for their draw.

We were still number one in the world but it was clear other teams were now getting closer and catching us up. England could have narrowly managed to either draw or even win the series in 1990 while Pakistan had drawn home and away with us. More often than not we were still meeting the challenges facing us but there were signs that our empire might not last for ever. The Aussies arrived in the Caribbean in early 1991 for what was a riveting series between two great teams. Australia were number two according to the rankings so there was plenty to play for. David Boon's hundred in the weather-affected first Test (that was drawn in Jamaica) demonstrated they had come for a fight. Boon was a tough cricketer who I admired over the years. He was one of the few guys who could take it. By that I mean it never mattered what you threw at him as a bowler, he was never going to surrender; he was as tough as they come. The man didn't talk. The most he would do to interact with you was, if the ball went past his outside edge, he might just give you a slight nod of approval. He never showed any signs of weakness. There were other guys I played against and knew after working them over that you could look in their eyes and see that they were not so comfortable. You knew it was only a matter of time before you got them out. David Boon? Whether he was struggling, or uncomfortable or nervous, you would never ever know. He was not the most attractive of batsmen: there are some batsmen you would line up to see because they're so elegant, but he was not one of those, though he got the job done.

Our own Gus Logie showed some guts, too, at Sabina Park after he was struck under the right eye by a Craig McDermott bouncer. He retired hurt on nine but returned to score 77 not out after we were up against it at 75 for six. When Logie came off with his cheek wide open, we all thought that was the match for him. We were wrong. He went back out to bat when many batsmen would have stayed in the pavilion. That tells you about the character of Gus Logie and the kind of toughness and fight that he had in him. He was a little lad with a big heart and his courage in that innings exemplified the spirit of that West Indies team in those days. We would have had to break a leg or arm to come off the field. Even when Malcolm Marshall did break an arm he still batted, one-handed with his broken arm in a sling in 1984. Viv continued to foster that never-say-die attitude. That's what our cricket was all about.

Jamaica also gave me my first close-up view of Mark Waugh. I thought he was very elegant, unlike his brother Steve. Mark had more talent and had more time to play his shots; he was like Carl Hooper in terms of being easy on the eye. But I will tell you that Steve Waugh had a huge heart and was a tough nut and would fight, fight, fight to the end. As good as Mark Waugh was I always felt he could be rattled easily and I have done it, usually with a few short balls. If you were aggressive with him he became a different character and tried to counter-attack, which is not really his game. He could be intimidated. After a while he would throw in the towel. I think he might even agree with me. Steve Waugh on the other hand, no, he would jump and hop and skip and look out of sorts and you felt, 'Yeah, I've got him', but you hadn't. They were two very different kinds of player. We won the second and fourth Tests to take a 2-0 lead into the fifth match in Antigua. There, Mark Waugh scored a good hundred – but I still intimidated him. As I went after him with a few short ones, he started to back away and slash over the slips and third man area. Viv said, 'Come on, Big Fella, he doesn't like it, he doesn't fancy it.' He was in the nineties when he started playing those shots. Over the years I found batsmen became more cautious at that stage. But the more aggressive I got with Mark the more he backed away and wasn't getting in line. It was out of character and he was certainly intimidated. I intimidated him quite a lot over the years. To be fair to him, he still got runs also, but he always looked suspect when I bowled to him. A lot of other guys were the same, though, as I was not an easy guy to negotiate.

We won the second Test in Guyana by ten wickets. Richie bossed the game with a spectacular 182. A dangerous player, Richie was not spoken of enough. He was underrated. After all, nine of his sixteen Test hundreds were against Australia, which tells you something about him. Even the great Viv Richards only scored five against the Australians – and in more matches. Richie made runs against the best. It was just unfortunate for him that when commentators speak about the great West Indies batsmen of that era you hear Greenidge and Haynes, you hear Richards, you hear Lloyd, but rarely do people speak of Richardson. Even when Lloyd, Greenidge, Richards and Dujon retired, along came the new sensation, Brian Lara, and stole the spotlight that looked destined to shine on Richie. So he was unlucky in terms of the adulation he received, or didn't receive. In Guyana I took my one hundredth wicket in my twenty-fifth Test when Mark Waugh edged to Viv at slip. I never played for records but that achievement meant something to me: it gave me a sense of belonging to this game. I actually have a lot of history with Guyana as I made my first-class debut there, I played my first Test match there, took my first Test wicket there, got my 100th wicket in Guyana and I took my 200th there, too.

I can't mention the rain-affected bore draw in Trinidad without speaking of my one and only Test fifty! I put on 87 with Jeffrey Dujon after we had been really struggling at 110 for seven (ending up 227 all out). I felt very confident and always fancied myself with the bat but I gave it away in the end, trying to slap Mark Waugh over midwicket but was caught at mid-off. And I want to make it clear that I dominated that partnership, which means a lot as Dujon was a top-order batsman. He played second fiddle to *me*!

The fourth Test was all about Gordon Greenidge, whose 226 helped us to a comprehensive victory and with it a series win. Gordon was not scoring too many runs and around that time he started to wear his glasses. So people started to say, 'He's wearing glasses – he can't see properly', 'He's over the hill'. When we got to Barbados, he took out the limp and we all know what happened when Gordon took out the limp – he always scored runs. I don't know if it was deliberate or if he was in pain but we saw it from time to time and when the limp was out it was trouble for the bowlers. The fickleness of opinion reared its head again as one minute Gordon couldn't see, next minute he scored a double and he's great again. His greatness should never have been in doubt. Mark Waugh and Mark Taylor steered the Aussies to a consolation win in Antigua. It was another satisfying series win against our nearest challengers. I wasn't at my very best in the series but still managed eighteen wickets, to warm me up for another tour of England.

Beamers, Aggro and County Cricket

'Dermot Reeve looked at me as if to say, "Are you crazy?" So I thought,
"I don't like the way this guy is looking at me." So I bowled him a
second beamer . . . He started saying things like, "You could have killed
me, I have a family!" I thought, "You know what, you talk too much."
And I bowled him a third beamer'

My reputation will almost certainly rest on what I achieved for West Indies, but I hope my six seasons in county cricket as an overseas player with Northamptonshire left an impression with supporters and neutral observers of a hard-working, world-class fast bowler who was committed to the cause. I never took county cricket lightly and always looked to raise the team's standards. Unfortunately, despite my appreciation that the club put their faith in me as a rookie back in 1987, my feelings towards Northants are not as positive as people might think. The simple reason being, they never looked after me as well as I believe they should have. In fact, their conduct towards me was at times disrespectful considering I was the number one ranked bowler in the world for much of the time I was associated with them. For the whole of my Northants career from 1989 to 1996 I felt undervalued. Yet they always turned to me to bail them out of all kinds of situations when the team wasn't doing well. They knew I did my best for them on each and every day I played county cricket, but my honest toil was not rewarded as it should have been.

Northants first approached me in 1987 through their chief executive, Steve Coverdale, after I had taken 115 wickets for Heywood in the Central Lancashire League. The plan was for me to play in 1988, but when I was picked for West Indies that year it was put back to '89. When I reflect, I played for Northamptonshire for six seasons and was never once paid what I was worth. I have never moaned about it as I am a professional and did my job and I did it well. I never had an agent and generally accepted what they offered me. At first I was just happy to be offered a county contract as there was a certain amount of prestige associated with that. My first contract was worth just £4,000 for the 1988 season but when I couldn't play it was increased to £11,900 for 1989 after I had become a West Indies international. For the 1990, 1992 and 1993 seasons, my pay hovered around the £23,000 mark. The money increased marginally for my final two county campaigns in 1994 and 1996 to just over £30,000. The club could have done much more for me. I knew I deserved more and even after I had toured England twice in 1988 and 1991, and after my eight for 45 against them in 1990, I was still never paid my worth. It's difficult to say what my worth was but my value was far higher than their salaries would suggest. And my grievances with Northants do not just emanate from pay issues, which I will expand on.

After three or four seasons with them, when I was at the top of the world rankings, I began to reflect and thought, 'Man, these people are paying me a pittance.' But any time I raised the subject with them they didn't really want to know. I'm a fair and reasonable man and wasn't asking for a lot of money. Income tax took care of a sizeable chunk out of my already minimal wage so I was left with almost nothing. I asked them one year to pay me enough on top of my typical wage that would effectively take care of the tax. They refused. Anytime I wanted something that would be a mere token of appreciation they refused, and I always accepted it. Before the 1994 county season, I had just finished a real tough five-match Test series with England that we won 3-1. The club called me in Antigua to say they wanted me to fly back with the England team two days later to start the season. I was already losing interest because of the way they were treating me and I thought, 'I'm not jumping on no damn plane two days after a hard series.' All I wanted and all I had asked for was one week's rest at home to relax and recharge the batteries. They didn't even accept that. I didn't go when they had asked me and, although I was wrong to stay back as I was under contract, all I wanted was a week's rest so that I could do my job for them properly. Nowadays the home board would probably block the player from going, full stop. They were pushing me to go back just to play a Benson & Hedges Cup game against Middlesex – five days after the England series had finished.

Newspaper stories came out with headlines to the theme of 'Ambrose Goes Missing', 'Ambrose Gone AWOL'. It looked like I was the bad guy when all I wanted was seven days while I was jaded. In the end I offered to fly a little earlier if they upped the ante and paid me a bit more; because the pittance they were paying me was starting to bother me. When I arrived I was greeted by a million photographers. The club made me look bad when someone there could have told the media about my fatigue and that I needed one week off. I went and played for no extra but I promised myself that year was to be my last in county cricket. And the game at Lord's in the B&H Cup? They lost. I also missed the first four-day game against Leicester, which they also lost.

They offered me another contract for 1996, after I toured England with West Indies in '95. I said 'No'. They kept calling me and I thought to myself, 'You're a professional, you should go.' So I went even though they pathetically insisted they couldn't pay me any more money. I am honest enough to admit that my heart was not in the club that year. But don't hear me wrong: once I walk on the field I am putting in 100 per cent because I am a proud man and my reputation is on the line. I still wanted to win. I took forty-three wickets in nine games so it is not like I wasn't putting it in. But I simply wasn't as passionate as I used to be; I would be more supportive in the dressing room before, saying words like, 'Come on, guys, we gotta do this, we gotta do that.' But in '96 I sat back more. I had fallen out of love with the club.

My grievances at Wantage Road were not all financial. For starters, it took the club two full seasons to award me my

Kent Libraries,
Registration and Archives
www.kent.gov.uk/libraries
Tel: 03000 41 31 31

Items that you have borrowed

Title: Curtly Ambrose : time to talk
ID: C3339260a4
Due: 24 August 2023

Title: Elevation
ID: C3344545361
Due: 24 August 2023

Total items: 2
Account balance: £0.00
Borrowed: 4
Overdue: 0
Reservation requests: 0
Ready for collection: 0
03/08/2023 11:29

Thank you for using self service

county cap, after I scored 55 not out and took twelve wickets at Leicestershire. I was surprised and disappointed not to be awarded my county cap much earlier. That, to me, was disrespectful because it suggested I had not performed for the best part of two seasons. Many lesser players had received theirs much sooner. I wasn't always looked after with other non-cricket issues either. I complained about the food so many times but nothing was ever done to rectify my complaints. I wanted hot food at lunch, or just food that I enjoyed, but most of the time they prepared cold meat platters, which were very bland. When we were on the road at different counties I knew that I would have to pick around what was there but when we were playing at Wantage Road I expected to be fed properly. The food was poor for my entire six seasons and on many occasions I had to leave the ground on my own just to fetch something I wanted. Sometimes I would even leave in my whites if we were in the field, at a time when I should have had my feet up. I was not asking for anything out of the ordinary; I just wanted something tasty and hot, not cold sandwiches or salads every day. It was just another example of how they never looked after me. This was brought home to me in '96 when I read somewhere that the club bent over backwards to accommodate the culinary preferences of Indian spinner Anil Kumble, their overseas player in my absence in '95.

There were many other things that soured my time at the club. In my last season of '96, after Kumble had been bowled into the ground the year prior for his 105 wickets, there were a few comments that annoyed me. I read some quotes from people on the Northants staff or committee along the lines of

'No offence to other overseas players we have had but Kumble really made a difference, blah, blah.' When I read that I felt extremely disrespected, as though I was worth nothing. But I didn't say anything because I don't like confrontation, unless I'm pushed into a corner and there's no getting away from it. I thought to myself, 'I've worked my arse off for this club for years, had no injuries, I'm always on the park, I've always been underpaid, hardly fed properly and despite all that I still got on with my job.' I was pleased for Kumble that he was given the means required to perform to his best, but it was another slap in the face for me. That really dampened my spirits and I was adamant I would not sign up for another season of county cricket after that. Not for Northants anyway.

Even a simple gesture about my club car was an issue. In my first season, while still a county rookie, I was given a new sponsored 1.4 Ford Escort. It was too small for a six-foot-eight fast bowler, but I didn't complain and appreciated the fact they arranged a new car for me. But it was all downhill from there. From my second year to my last at the club I had to make do with a beaten-up old used car with lots of miles on the clock. In 1993 I drove this cranky Vauxhall from my home in Northampton to Birmingham, as I was visiting a friend, and it broke down. A mechanic in Birmingham advised me it was a serious fault that needed rectifying so I had to call a tow truck to take me and my knackered car back to Northampton. The club never did pay me for those costs I incurred. It was all quite embarrassing for me. For my final two years I had a used Ford Sierra, which belonged to the chairman of the club, the late Lynn Wilson. It was kind of Lynn but yet another example of the penny-pinching attitude shown by the club towards its so-called overseas star player.

I enjoyed the guys in the Northants dressing room, despite my problems off the field. As in every dressing room there were players I connected with more than some. Allan Lamb and I have always got along well and had mutual respect for one another after our battles in international cricket. Lamby's a larger than life character and loved the social side of the game – more than most I've known. I also got along very well with David Capel and Nigel Felton. And the late Kevin Curran became a good friend when he left Courtney at Gloucester and decided to join 'the other half'. There were always things going on socially but I never did a lot in between games because there was so much cricket that I liked to rest, put my feet up, watch some telly and listen to some music. If I did do anything it was usually meeting up with friends or just going out for lunch or dinner with Bridget, who would always accompany me during my county seasons. There was never anything too exciting going on. I have heard the clichés about how travelling cricketers have a girl in every port but that's not me. It is true that many women are attracted to athletes, but in my case I had my girlfriend with me at every opportunity. That's not to say, though, that I didn't receive my fair share of attention from female admirers, because I did and I enjoyed it very much. Why not? I'm a man. I still have female admirers now – and *still* enjoy the attention!

As far as the cricket goes, it was a very tough baptism for me with Northants back in 1989. I didn't bowl all that well at first and I had expected to come straight in and be an instant success; my twenty-eight wickets at an average of 28.39 shows that I was anything but an instant success. The routine of playing almost every day and travelling to the different counties was a bit taxing and not something I was accustomed to. Myself and fellow West Indies quick Winston Davis shared the workload that season and again in 1990. I said to Nick Cook at the end of that first season, 'This is a learning process for me. When I come back next year you're going to see a different Curtly Ambrose.' I was trying too hard in that first season, though I had only been in international cricket eighteen months, so I was still learning the art of fast bowling. We got to the NatWest Trophy final in 1990, losing to Lancashire, the one-day kings at the time. In fact, before that game Clive Lloyd, who was the manager of West Indies at the time, called me up and said, 'Ambi, we're good friends but you can't get past Lancashire, they're my boys.' Me and David Capel both got run out after we had dragged the team back into it after being 56 for six. Clive was ultimately right – we couldn't get past Lancashire. There was at least a trophy to shout about in 1992 when we won the NatWest against Winston Benjamin's Leicestershire. By this time I felt I had arrived in world cricket and already had some decent exposure in county cricket by then.

My driving force was always to help Northants win the County Championship because they had never won that (and still haven't), but sadly we were unable to do so despite threatening once or twice, like in 1994. I wanted people to say Curtly Ambrose was worth the signing and helped them go that extra mile to win the competition. After six years it didn't happen, though I thought it might have been our year in '94 but unfortunately there was a 'no-good' batsman up the M6 called Brian Charles Lara, who powered Warwickshire to three trophies that year. He didn't do it alone but because of his exploits with the bat he took the team to another level. We also tailed off that season but it was one of my best years in county cricket (77 wickets at 14.45). There was this big hype as I was the number one bowler in the world and Brian was the number one batsman, having just come off his world record-breaking 375 in Antigua and the 501 also. Almost every English newspaper wanted to know about this showdown and who would win this contest between the two of us. Every paper you picked up was about our rivalry: 'Lara in the blue corner against Ambrose in the red corner'. They were interviewing people like Carl Hooper, who was over with Kent. Everyone was giving their opinion. I grew tired of the hype and thought to myself, 'I'm going to tell the club that I'm not playing this game against Warwickshire', because I didn't like the hype. Then I thought about it some more and concluded that if I didn't play this game they would all say Ambrose is frightened of Lara and I'm running from him. I was too proud to allow that to happen. I knew Lara was a great batsman but I felt I was good enough to keep him quiet, so I decided I would play.

Two of my good friends, Stuart Williams and Kenny Benjamin, were in England at the time playing in the leagues and they came down to watch the duel and stayed at my house for the whole match. It was a contest worth waiting for. Ultimately none of us had anything to prove as we had both proved ourselves at the highest level anyway. Brian scored 197 but my good friend Kevin Curran dropped him at slip off my bowling before he had three figures. I also bowled him a bouncer that hit him on his helmet, which caused Kenny to shout from the sidelines, 'None of that, we need him', because we were touring India later that year. I backed off after that and didn't get him out. The papers declared it a drawn match because, although I didn't get him out he was dropped off me, I hit him on his helmet and he only scored nine runs off me in forty-three deliveries. No boundaries either. I thought I won the contest because of the dropped catch, the crack on the helmet and so few runs off my bowling. But I was happy to accept what the press said about our contest.

It's interesting that one of my other most memorable games in county cricket also involved Warwickshire. Many will remember it as the game in which I bowled three consecutive beamers at the highly annoying Dermot Reeve. I never really bowled beamers to batsmen as that's not professional. That was not how I did my thing. But the incident with Reeve was an exception. The Northampton guys produced a really flat pitch because Warwickshire had in their ranks Allan Donald, who was genuinely quick. They shaved all the grass off to dampen Donald's pace. I was very upset about it. I said to our skipper Lamby and the guys in the team, 'What about me? I am very upset about this', and was close to not playing. I said, 'How can you be thinking about Donald? I'm here. If Donald is good enough to bowl us out on a sporty pitch then I am too. You have to give me a chance. You want me to win games for the club but then you give me a flat-ass pitch like that!'

I was totally irate about their attitude. I was so upset that I cannot remember their response – though I did most of the talking. So we played the game and Reeve batted very well for his 200. But in doing so he was charging down the pitch to some of our guys, though he played me as he would normally. I watched him taking these liberties with our bowlers and I didn't like it. You can understand it in a one-day game but this was a four-day match. I was already upset with the Northants staff over the pitch, so when Reeve started doing this charging, I wasn't having it. So when I came on to bowl I figured, 'I need to send a clear message to this guy that you are not going to do that to me.' So I bowled him an intentional beamer. I couldn't make my point with a short ball as there was nothing happening in the pitch.

I did not bowl it with the intention of hurting him and it wasn't dangerous as it was way over his head but I felt it important I made a statement to Reeve that he should not even think about charging me. He looked at me as if to say, 'Are you crazy?' So I thought, 'I don't like the way this guy is looking at me.' So I bowled him a second beamer – again way over his head. He started saying things like, 'You could have killed me, I have a family!' I thought, 'You know what, you talk too much.' And I bowled him a third beamer. This time, he said nothing. Lamby came up to me and tried to cool me down: 'Come on, King [which is what they called me there], settle down.' I realised also I wasn't in the right frame of mind and took a break from the attack.

The Warwickshire people were telling the papers later that they were going to report me to Lord's. I didn't mind; I figured if they wanted to ban me I would just jump on a plane back to Antigua. It all settled down, though. But afterwards a story got out that us West Indies fast bowlers had a thing against Dermot Reeve as I think he was also roughed up by Courtney at Gloucestershire and Winston Benjamin at Leicestershire. I also heard, while all this was going on that in the next game we played against Warwickshire, that Dermot Reeve asked Allan Donald to give me some of my own treatment but Donald refused to get involved. For the record, we never had anything against Reeve.

There were many good memories at Northants but the off-field issues were highly disappointing. But even with all that negative history, and even though my passion for Northants had seriously been watered down, I still came close to signing again for the 1998 season – but not without the usual pantomime that again demonstrated their lack of respect for me. During the England series in the Caribbean in '98, John Emburey, who was then the club coach, said they wanted me back. I explained that I did not really fancy returning again. But then he told me that Kevin Curran was going to be the new captain and that he really wanted me to be the overseas player and felt I could make the difference and help us win something. That was one of the few things that Emburey could have said to interest me as I got along very well with Curran, a Zimbabwean. If it was not for Curran I could not even have considered it. The more I thought about it the more I convinced myself that I would give Curran one year, because of our friendship. But before I could accept and sign up I heard a strong rumour from a very credible source that the club had offered Shane Warne £120,000 to play the '98 season. Now imagine how I felt at this time, especially as I was not even on half of that money. Warney was apparently blocked from signing by the Australian Cricket Board, as it was then, so the club came back to me. I thought, 'All these years I have been with the club, I've been the number one bowler in the world and they've never given me half of that.'

My mind was made up, I wasn't going, despite my friendship with Curran. But Embers came back to me and I thought, 'OK, I will have a talk.' I told him I had heard about the Warne story and he put me in touch with Steve Coverdale straight away as he couldn't make executive decisions or get involved on finance. I told Coverdale, 'I've heard you were prepared to pay Shane Warne £120,000, OK. I understand he's a better bowler than me, he will bowl more overs and therefore has the chance to take more wickets than me. I'm a realist. So I will come for £100,000 – save the club £20,000.' He laughed and explained that the offer to Warne was based on sponsorship money. So I suggested the club find the sponsorship money for me instead. He laughed again so I told him I would be prepared to come for £80,000. He still wasn't having it: 'You know we can't afford to pay you that money.' But they could afford it for Shane Warne! So I gave him one last chance and said, 'Look, OK, I will come for half of that money, £60,000.' He still wasn't prepared to pay me half of what they had offered Shane Warne so I said, 'Am I only half as good as Shane Warne? Forget it. Don't call me again.'

I was angry. After six seasons bowling my heart out for the club they still expected me to keep signing on for a meagre salary. Agents might not be appreciated by everyone but at least players would not be exploited like I was back then. I enjoyed the spectators and the guys in the dressing room, but I am afraid those negative experiences did sour me towards the club. I felt I deserved a lot better over the years. It was a sad end.

The Beginning of the End?

'We worked [Graeme Hick] out and realised he didn't like the short ball
– he wasn't a good hooker and was more of a front foot player who liked
to drive a lot. He was a decent player but the pressure took its toll on
him. I always fancied my chances against Hick'

The England tour in 1991 was a watershed for West Indies cricket and it could be safely argued this was the time when the signs of our eventual decline first became apparent. For me this tour was another opportunity to continue my ascent in international cricket as I began to stamp my name among the best fast bowlers around. But for West Indies the tour represented a period of huge change. The fifth Test at The Oval was the last for Viv Richards, Malcolm Marshall and Jeffrey Dujon, while we would never again see Gordon Greenidge in the baggy maroon either. How can any team lose such four greats as those and continue to dominate? The simple answer . . . it can't. That we managed to carry on as number one for another four years was a testimony to the guys who remained and the youngsters who came in like

Brian Lara, Jimmy Adams and Shivnarine Chanderpaul. But, if not before now, this period really was the obvious time when the West Indies Cricket Board should have identified the need to reinvest in our cricket and nurture the talent beneath the top level. They never looked to develop the next generation enough. While Australia built academies, we did nothing and instead allowed complacency to creep in rather than going for regeneration, thinking we would always produce great cricketers – but it doesn't work like that.

By 1991 I didn't consider myself a rookie any more. I was still learning but had matured and knew a lot more about fast bowling. I was primed and pumped up to go forward in my career. England beat us in the first Test at Headingley, comfortably. I didn't know it at the time but I since learned it was England's first win against us in a home Test since 1969. We never looked at stats too much then; it was all about winning. England captain Graham Gooch stroked 154 not out in the second innings for what was a great innings against a top-class West Indies attack. The ball was nipping around a bit and he played very well and that knock was the difference between us winning or losing. I must say we thought we had him caught behind early on but the umpire didn't give him. Had we got that decision it would have been all over. But we could have been wrong so I don't want to complain too much. Credit to Gooch as the conditions favoured fast bowling and he held the innings together on his own. I took the first six wickets in England's second dig but there were no thoughts of anything crazy happening, like all ten. I never thought like that.

Headingley was also a significant match because it witnessed the Test debut of Graeme Hick – the player who was supposed to take us apart like he had every county team. We well remembered that big hundred he scored against us at Worcester in 1988. While I was playing county cricket in '89 and '90 I could detect this great hype that Hick was going to be some kind of knight in shining armour for England – the saviour of English cricket. So in '91 he was one of our big targets, for two reasons. One, because we hadn't forgotten his innings at Worcester, which we didn't like too much – it was a great innings; and, two, because of all the hype. We thought, 'No, sorry, but you're going to have to wait to deliver against some other team, not the West Indies.' He was really under the microscope and a guy we were looking to take out. Indeed, he ended up having a poor series and was dropped for the final game. It was still a very strong West Indies team after all. The problem that he faced, apart from the obvious force of our team, was the tremendous pressure he was under right through his qualifying period. It was never going to be easy for him. They batted him at three and that was the right thing to do as that was where he batted for Worcestershire, but he simply failed and couldn't survive the huge pressure he was under.

We never had any video analysis in those days so we sat and discussed how we were going to get him out. We worked him out and realised he didn't like the short ball – he wasn't a good hooker and was more of a front foot player who liked to drive a lot. I always fancied my chances against Hick. Whenever we met I was up for the challenge and wanted to get the best of him, and usually I succeeded. It was nothing to do with a lack of ability; he just didn't cope with the pressure very well. He was a beaten man by the time of the fourth Test and I had dismissed him six times out of seven. We weren't a big sledging team but when Viv sensed weakness in the opposition he perked up. With Hick, Viv would say things like, 'Here's your man, Big Fella', 'He doesn't want it, he's ready to surrender.' Some guys like Gooch, Lamby and Robin Smith would suck it in and try to prove us wrong but others would falter. I kept saying to the guys that I had lost two wickets when he was dropped for the final Test at The Oval. I never judged him, though, as I knew he would get better with time. But the selectors did him some damage by dropping him quite a lot over his career. Likewise with another they gave a debut to in that match – Mark Ramprakash. Ramps got some starts, got a few twenties without going on. Desi Haynes, who was his Middlesex team-mate, used to say when Ramps would get towards twenty-five, 'Be sharp now, guys, he's got his quota.'

We came back to 1-1 at Trent Bridge in the third Test after rain had forced a draw at Lord's. I took eight in Nottingham so my rhythm was in good order. The fourth Test in Birmingham was significant for two reasons: one, we won to lead the series 2-1. But two, I saw one of the most intelligent and brilliant exhibitions of fast bowling ever, with Malcolm Marshall giving me a masterclass in the art. If you cannot learn from exponents like Malcolm then you shouldn't be playing the game.

Maco is the greatest we have produced and he was head of the crop: the best fast bowler in the world. As I've said, he had a great cricket brain – he understood fast bowling and was more than just a good competitor. Many times I would be standing at mid-off and he would tell me what he was going to bowl and he would then do it. He didn't do that to show off; that was Maco's way of teaching us the tricks of the trade. He took his role as the senior fast bowler in the team very seriously. Malcolm would even ask us questions. In that fourth Test at Edgbaston, he was swinging and seaming the ball all over the place and Graham Gooch could not lay a bat on him. He was unplayable and I was enjoying the show, thinking, 'I can't wait for my turn.' Then he turned to me and said, 'How you think I'm going to get him out, Ambi?' My immediate answer was, 'Caught behind or in the slip cordon', and he said, 'No.' I thought, 'Marshall's got to be crazy, why wouldn't he get him caught as it's only a matter of time before Gooch nicks one?' Maco said, 'I can't get him out like that, the ball is doing too much. I am going to bowl him down.' He explained that Gooch was looking for outswingers all the time so he would bowl him an inswinger. I walked away thinking that's madness. A few balls later Gooch went for this big drive and was bowled between bat and pad. Maco set him up and surprised him with an inswinger. I thought to myself, 'Wow, this man knows about fast bowling.' I was only in my third year of Test cricket and I would have persisted with those outswingers, making Gooch look silly as I liked the whole show. I put my hands up and said to Maco, 'You're the King.' And he did it all the time.

West Indies opening batsman Gordon Greenidge played with Marshall at Hampshire, as well as Barbados and West Indies, and he acknowledged the impact he had on young Curtly. 'Malcolm was a great conman with the ball; he would sucker the batsman in and then lay him out flat. I'm sure he was a

good influence on Curtly. Because Malcolm was able to do the things he was
teaching, when he said something, people listened.'

At The Oval, Viv received a great reception from the crowd in his last appearance, with Marshall and Dujon also bowing out then, too. There were no 'thanks for the memories' speeches in the dressing room because, though he was finished in Test cricket, he wanted to play the World Cup in Australia a few months later. That was going to be his swansong, to go there as a batsman only and not as captain. England's rookie left-arm spinner Phil Tufnell cleaned us up with six for 25 in our first innings and we never came back. We played some irresponsible shots against him, as West Indies teams of that era relied on confidence, but we were probably overconfident against Tufnell and we tried to show him who's boss a bit too early and suffered the consequences. He took six for four in thirty-three balls. We didn't play him well and were not at all cautious against him. We tried to hit Tufnell out of the attack and there were some ill-advised shots. It was a painful loss and earned England a fighting 2-2 series draw. We did not, though, feel this was the end of an era. We knew there was a big void to fill with those greats leaving the team but we felt we had enough players to continue our winning trend. And we showed that as we went another four years before Australia took our number one status.

Not that our 1992 World Cup showing reflected that faith. We crashed out of that tournament miserably, failing to reach the semi-finals after coming sixth in the nine-team league. This was my first World Cup and it was highly disappointing. I am

not going to say that with the inclusion of Viv, Jeffrey Dujon
and Courtney Walsh we would have won the World Cup,
because you never know with one-day cricket, but with those
guys we would have been a stronger team and our chances
would have been better. One happier memory I have of that
rather forgettable World Cup was the win over India and
taking the wicket of a young Sachin Tendulkar. I had him
caught behind for just four but I already knew by then he was
destined for greatness. I had been playing county cricket in
1990 when he scored a brilliant hundred at Old Trafford. I
remember watching it and saying to myself, 'You should be in
school! Not playing Test cricket.' But I recognised the amount
of talent he possessed at that age. So when I played against
him in that World Cup I thought, 'Here's a young man, full of
talent. I am the elder statesman so it's important I stamp my
authority on this youngster.' I said to the guys that I can't have
this rookie take me to pieces. I brought my A game and he was
dropped by the wicketkeeper David Williams, two balls before
I got him. I was not surprised to see him score all those runs in
his career. The thing that impressed me most was how humble
he remained throughout his years of success.

Not long after we returned from the World Cup we were
preparing to face South Africa in their first game back in
international cricket, which was a big occasion for them after
twenty-two years in the wilderness. A lot of great South
African cricketers never had the opportunity to play Test
matches in that time because of politics and it was really sad
that they never had their chance to showcase their skills on the
world stage. I saw this game as a bit of a joke in that it was only

a one-off match. That was dangerous for us with our world number one reputation to protect. There should have been three matches, minimum two. If you lose the first Test any team should have the opportunity to come back. If South Africa won that game, were they the best team in the world all of a sudden? It was crazy. A one-off Test proved nothing to us or them.

We began that game in Barbados in extremely hostile circumstances. There was a boycott because Anderson Cummins, who had done well in a few one-day matches but had not played a Test, was left out of this match in favour of Kenny Benjamin, who also hadn't played a Test and came in for his debut. He made up the pace attack along with myself, Courtney and Patrick Patterson. There was no comparison between Kenny and Anderson Cummins. I and the whole of the Caribbean knew Kenny was the better fast bowler but this did not placate the Bajans, who were disappointed that Desmond Haynes was the only Bajan in the team. So we started on the back foot. They kept their protest up through the whole of the match and the attendance was minimal. I lost some respect for the Bajan spectators through this episode because it meant they cared more for their local interests than for West Indies cricket. I thought that showed an insular attitude and although I've long since moved on, at that point I thought it was grossly disrespectful towards West Indies cricket.

We struggled in that game and they had us on the ropes for much of the time. It didn't look good for us as Kepler Wessels was scenting a landmark victory for his South Africa team. In those days you got a rest day after three days. And on the rest day some local officials arranged a boat cruise for both teams. You should have seen the South Africans partying and having fun. The music was playing and they were having a wonderful time but they were in the driving seat at that stage so they had every right to be happy. But we were in a sombre mood and didn't want to party too much because we were behind the eight ball. I am not saying they should not have partied but their laughter and enjoyment translated to us as a message that they felt they had already won. Jimmy Adams then played a great knock for his 79 not out, after his four wickets on debut. The game came down to South Africa needing 79 runs on the final day with eight wickets in hand. I took the two wickets on the fourth evening to give us a sniff but we were struggling to dismiss the veterans Wessels and Peter Kirsten. On a fifth-day pitch things were always going to happen but we needed to plan accordingly and ensure we gave ourselves every chance of snatching an unlikely win.

On the evening before that final day we had a discussion. The general theme was that we could not afford to lose given that it was South Africa's first Test match in twenty-one years and it would be embarrassing for us to lose to them because they were a rookie team. They were all on debut apart from Wessels, so we figured, 'We can't have a bunch of rookies beating us – we're the best in the world.' Despite the adversity we were up against, our attitude was, 'There's no way we're going to lose to South Africa.' And I remember Desmond Haynes saying in the meeting, 'No matter what, Curtly Ambrose and Courtney Walsh have to bowl for the whole day.

If we're going to lose, we're going to lose with those two bowlers trying their hearts out. If we're going to win, it will be those guys who will do it for us.'

Haynes recalled: 'That was agreed by the whole team. But as we resumed the following morning Richie told Patrick Patterson to warm up. I said to Richie, "What you doing, that's not the plan?" Richie got outvoted and we went with the original plan and it worked beautifully.'

Patrick Patterson wasn't having a good game and Kenny was on debut and couldn't be trusted with any responsibility in those tight situations. I noticed that after Malcolm Marshall left the scene it became all about Courtney Walsh and Curtly Ambrose in terms of us trying to lift the team, trying to drag the young guys through. And you could see on the boys' faces on days when we were not on top of our games a look of concern: 'Oh boy, we're in trouble here with Ambi and Cuddy not performing.' And it worked in the other way, too, that when we were bowling well in tandem, it lifted the whole team. I am not saying the other guys couldn't take wickets, but myself and Courtney were just depended upon so much. So when we went out to bowl, South Africa were 122 for two, chasing 201 for victory. Wickets began to fall almost immediately and I ended up with six for 34 (in 24.4 overs) and Courtney took four for 31. Our debutant wicketkeeper David Williams took a brilliant catch off the inside edge of Adrian Kuiper's bat from Courtney and that really settled the match. They ended up losing those eight wickets for just twenty-six runs. This was another example of the team's greatness, when you are able to withstand such pressure when all seems lost and still find a way to win. That is greatness. This was one of my most treasured victories, along with the one-run win against Australia in Adelaide in 1992–93.

The Greatest Spell of All Time

'There was no one in world cricket at that time who could have subdued me. Not even Sir Donald Bradman in his pomp'

By 12.58 p.m. on the third day of the fifth and final Test against Australia in Perth, the match and the series were over. West Indies were triumphant by an innings and twenty-five runs, taking the series 2-1 and sending out a clear statement to our rivals that we were far from a spent force and were still worthy of our world number one tag. So there was plenty on the line before that winner-takes-all clash in February 1993. That Test also witnessed one of the best spells of my career and what some commentators have described as the best spell ever bowled. Everything was set up beautifully, with the series poised, and for me personally there could not have been a better suited playing surface waiting for me. I had the added assurance that I had played at the WACA four years earlier and had picked up eight wickets in the match. So I knew what Perth was all about.

On the first morning of the match I looked at the pitch and said to our captain, Richie Richardson, that it looked 'ripe for fast bowling'. It wasn't green but it had some grass and moisture and was hard. 'Skipper,' I said, 'if you win this toss we will win the Test match and the series', because it was obvious we would bowl first. But what happened? Allan Border won the toss – and elected to bat first. Richie came back to the dressing room and I could hardly wait to find out what we were doing. 'They won the toss,' Richie said. I thought, 'Damn. We are going to have to bat well here!' And then Richie added, 'They are taking first knock.' I was shocked, totally surprised, and could not understand their decision. I'm not just saying it because we won the game but any team would have had to have bowled first on that pitch. It was a big mistake on Allan Border's part as we would have had a hard time negotiating Craig McDermott, Merv Hughes and Jo Angel on that surface. His decision was one hell of a gift to West Indies!

They actually started pretty well, reaching 59 for two at lunch. My first spell of 0 for 14 from eight overs was very ordinary. I did not quite get the line or the length right so they were able to leave a lot of deliveries. With the new ball as a fast bowler you want the batsman to play as many deliveries as possible. Ian Bishop had taken the two early wickets to fall – Justin Langer and Steve Waugh – and I was annoyed with myself that I did not get it right with the pitch so conducive to fast bowling. I came off at lunchtime very upset with myself because I felt I bowled badly. I mark myself hard because I strive for excellence and when things don't go right I am not a happy man. I still didn't go for many runs but I knew I had not made an impression on a pitch that suited my bowling. To emphasise the point, seventeen of my first eighteen balls in the match were dot balls, apart from a three by David Boon, but I just didn't threaten the stumps enough. Normally I am a guy who is able to switch off once I walk back into the dressing room and enjoy a bit of humour, before putting my game face back on again. But on this occasion I was really upset, especially after telling Richie how keen I was to bowl first. This was not a time for laughing or joking. I sat alone reflecting on the way I had bowled because I felt like I had wasted a whole session in which I hadn't done anything for the team. The guys knew when to let me be in the dressing room – this was one of those times – and I didn't say anything to anyone as this situation was nothing to do with the guys. I would normally let them have it if they messed up but this time it was me who had messed up. They knew not to interfere or chitchat with me until I was chilled out a little more. I was upset for the whole forty minutes of that lunch interval and was punishing myself. I thought, 'There is no way I am going to go back out after lunch and bowl like that again.' It was too good a pitch for me not to do better. By the time I had got my head right, I knew what I had to do and I was itching to go back.

Close friend and team-mate Courtney Walsh commented: 'When Curtly was angry with himself he never spoke much; he would go into a corner and think hard. During that lunch break, he was very disappointed with himself because the wicket was a good one for fast bowling and he hadn't bowled that well – in what was a deciding Test match. I kept saying to him that he had a long spell *in Adelaide and needed to be more patient. When he came back after lunch he produced the best spell of fast bowling that I was privileged to see – and I've seen a few while playing with Malcolm Marshall, Michael Holding, Joel Garner and Patrick Patterson. But that spell was something special. It was awesome to be a part of.'*

Richie came up to me just before the restart and asked me how I was feeling. 'Ready to bowl,' came my reply. The anger had now passed and I was all set to go again as I knew I could do better. There was no way I wasn't going to start the bowling after lunch as I could not have waited another hour for my second chance to threaten the Australian batsmen. Over my career, if I said to the captain, 'I want to bowl', there are very few times they would say 'No'. Even Viv; they knew when I was in the mood to do some damage and this was one of those occasions. So by the time I went out there I was focused and everything fell into place, and I settled on a line of off stump or just outside and just short of a length. I got Mark Waugh caught behind in my fourth over after lunch with a ball he could not help but nibble at just outside off stump (that was 85 for three). That set the tone and from there I could do no wrong. With the last two deliveries of my next over, I managed to have the stubborn and gutsy David Boon caught by Richie at a wide third slip (90 for four). He was on 44 and that was a big, big wicket. Then in came the great Allan Border. But he was gone first ball, caught by the wicketkeeper again, to one that lifted sharply and left him on off stump (90 for five). I didn't achieve the hat-trick, with Damien Martyn on strike, but I was still in the zone. Martyn took a single off the third ball of that over, which was a significant run in that spell of seven for one. There was no one in world cricket at that time who could have subdued me. Not even Sir Donald Bradman in his pomp, or Sir Viv Richards or Sir Garfield Sobers. I was unstoppable. Everything was perfect. Ian Healy went next, pushing outside off stump and was caught by Brian Lara at first slip (100 for six). Merv Hughes followed, as Keith Arthurton held a skier at cover after Merv tried to play a big shot over the top (102 for seven). That was my fifth wicket – and I wasn't done yet. Martyn was caught by Phil Simmons at second slip while driving on the up, again on an off-stump line (104 for eight), before debutant Jo Angel edged another on off stump to wicketkeeper Junior Murray for a duck (104 for nine). Shane Warne was the last man to go, run out, after he tried his luck with a few big shots, hitting three boundaries in one over from Courtney.

I finished with seven for 25, after 0 for 14 prior to lunch. It was the spell of my life: seven wickets for one run in thirty-two deliveries, with Australia all out for just 119. For pure rhythm it has to be tops, but I rate it fourth in terms of importance to the match situation as it was day one. My eight for 45 in Barbados and my six for 24 in Trinidad (both against England) and the six for 34 against South Africa in Barbados were more crucial to the results of those games, which were all won. Maybe you could argue the seven for 25 effectively decided this Perth Test as early as day one, but there was still a lot of cricket to be played.

West Indies opener Desmond Haynes recalled: 'Watching a guy bowl at that level where it looked like he was going to get a wicket with every ball – that to

me is phenomenal. That is not normal. It was clear that it was only a matter
of time before he bowled those guys out.'

Once we bowled the Australians out we felt we were going to win the game. Although we scored 322 for a lead of over 200, I wasn't happy about it because we were bowled out on the second day. I was upset and I told the guys in no uncertain terms that I expected to put my feet up for at least two days. It was a good pitch to bowl on but we should have applied ourselves better, I felt we should have batted for at least two days and scored somewhere nearer 500. Instead, though we had a decent lead I still felt like we had given them a sniff. If they had performed much better in their second innings things could have been different. But it wasn't to be. Ian Bishop took six for 40 and we rolled them again for an innings victory inside three days. I finished with nine in the match but it should have been ten as Phil Simmons dropped a slip catch to deny me. Ultimately it didn't matter.

People have asked me over the years what my secret formula is for bowling at the WACA and the simple answer is, there is no secret. There seems to be this fallacy that because it's Perth and because it's fast and bouncy you have to bowl short. Well, I hardly bowled any bouncers in that game; there was no need for them. I bowled too short before lunch on day one and I didn't trouble them. Some length balls even bounced over the stumps. But when I made the adjustment my success came. Too many bowlers get carried away with the bounce at Perth. You have to find what some people call the 'Perth-fect length'. I have more often than not managed to find that length, as the wickets in this match would support, with most being caught behind the wicket or at slip.

This series win ranks as the best of my career. Why? Because of the team we had. It was a team half full of rookies and no one gave us any chance of beating Australia in Australia. In previous series we were always expected to win with the playing strength we had. But with no Richards, Greenidge, Marshall or Dujon, and with Richardson still an inexperienced captain with just one Test behind him, this is easily my number one. We had a camp prior to this tour and throughout the camp we could tell there was not a great deal of support around, not from the public and especially not from officials. And that feeling came to the fore when we were due to depart for Australia from Barbados airport. There was not one member of the West Indies Cricket Board to see us off and wish us all the best, which was very unusual. Whenever we departed for a tour there was always a board official or two to see us off. But on this occasion only a lower-ranking liaison officer was there to see that we checked in OK et cetera. We were going on a huge tour with a young team and we expected our board to support us. It was clear to me that they stayed away because they had zero faith in us. I took that personally and was bitter about it.

We had a very young team with a few Test rookies like Jimmy Adams, Anderson Cummins, David Williams, Kenny Benjamin, Junior Murray and Phil Simmons, who had been around the team a fair while without playing much Test cricket. Even the young and talented Brian Lara had played only two Tests up to that point. So we were lacking the usual experience. The senior guys were myself, Walsh, Haynes, captain Richardson and Hooper. Even though we were still number one, no one gave us a chance against a very strong Australian team led by Allan Border. Everyone seemed to think this was the time our run would come to an end. I expected the Australians to say they were going to beat us – who would predict anything else? But even our own people in the Caribbean did not seem to give us a hope in hell.

We showed fight from the start. The first Test in Brisbane was a draw as Keith Arthurton, who had been around West Indies cricket for a while without really making a name for himself, scored 157 not out in what was a brilliant innings. He ended up having quite a good series with a couple of seventies also. Australia won the second Test, which was all about the emergence of a young leg-spinner by the name of Shane Warne, who took seven for 52 in our second innings. It was the first time I had the chance to look at him. He only took one wicket in the first innings – yours truly, caught at short midwicket. At that point we were not too concerned about him but he came back in the second innings and bowled Richie Richardson with one that kept low. That gave Warne some confidence and he got on a roll and the rot set in as far as we were concerned. He really bowled well and it wasn't a surprise when he went on to be a star because we recognised he had a talent for turning the ball quite sharply.

I believe the drawn third Test in Sydney was the match that changed the whole momentum of the series, courtesy of Brian Lara's incredible innings of 277. That double hundred changed our whole mentality on the tour. They couldn't get Brian out;

it was like they were bowling with a football. He was run out eventually. We started to talk about a world record in the dressing room. That day would come later for Brian, though. Richie scored a great hundred in that innings but no one remembers it because the match was dominated by Lara, a common theme in Richie's career. We went from a team that knew it could *compete* against a strong Australia to a team that knew it could *win*. It was very inspiring and more so because that inspiration came from a youngster. The older guys saw Brian's innings and thought it was time they too contributed and the rookies also began to think if Brian could make a difference like that so could they. Everyone might have expected a Haynes, a Richardson or a Hooper to play an innings like that, but for Lara to do it changed our whole thinking. The team was lifted and we then went and won everything after that, including the one-day series, thanks also to some ill-conceived intervention from Dean Jones. We played that fifty-over series between the third and fourth Tests and the now infamous 'wristband incident' is something I am asked about frequently.

It was the first final, at Sydney, and Australia were chasing 240 to win. They lost a couple of early wickets and Dean Jones came out. He hadn't even faced a delivery when umpire Terry Prue came to me and said Jones had asked that I remove my wristbands. My immediate reaction was 'Why? What's the problem?' The answer was something about the white ball clashing with the white wristbands. At first I thought he was joking. Anyone who has followed my career will know that I always wore wristbands, one on each arm, from day one to the day I retired. Initially they were red, gold and green but then the ICC made some rule that they had to be white. It was not a fashion thing for me. I used to sweat a lot and didn't want to get the ball wet and needed something dry to wipe my brow with. I also had a white rag tucked into my trousers, which I used to dry my fingers to stop the ball from slipping out of my hand. These items were simply part of my routine and up to that moment no one had ever had an issue with them. Dean Jones had faced me before with a white ball and my white wristbands but now all of a sudden he had a problem. I thought, 'No, I'm not going to do it. It is his problem.' I told the umpire it was a nonsense request and that I would not take them off. Richie and Ian Bishop saw what was happening and came over and agreed it was a strange request. We spent a few minutes discussing it as the guys tried to convince me for the sake of the game. Eventually I relented and took them both off and gave them to the umpire. I was furious. Up until then I was bowling well within myself and was trying to contain. One-day cricket is about containment and stopping the runs and in doing so taking wickets through building pressure. It is very simple. I attacked in Test matches, but in one-day cricket looked to keep the runs down.

After Jones's request, I thought: 'You should not have woken a sleeping lion.' I was so furious I started to bowl twice as fast and seriously wanted to knock Dean Jones out with the ball. I was really upset. I couldn't bowl too short because of the rules and regulations in one-day internationals but I still managed to send a few towards his ribcage and made his life pretty uncomfortable, though he negotiated me quite well. I didn't get him out but I didn't intend to; I just wanted to make his life uncomfortable for that stupid request.

What many people don't know is that when he was standing at the non-striker's end, maybe an over after he made his request, he said something to me while I was walking back to my mark. He spoke to me quietly, almost in a whisper, that if I wanted to put my wristbands back on he would not have a problem. He realised what was happening but by then it was too late to put the lion back to sleep. I thought, 'You've made your bed, brother; you're in some serious trouble now.' I finished with five for 32 and we won the game quite easily. I understand his team were not too happy with him and rightly so. I should have thanked him for motivating me.

It was a lesson learned for anyone who had designs on trying to rattle me. I never held a grudge against Jones and it wasn't mentioned again. That's how I operated. Things happen in battle and then you walk off the field and forget about them. I was more likely to remember a guy who scored a hundred against me so I could make sure it never happened again (as with Graeme Hick in 1988), than someone who was mouthing off. However, I have been known to remember the odd comment and one I can recall was from this tour. The debutant Justin Langer was asked after the game about a bouncer he missed from Ian Bishop in the fourth Test in Adelaide and he flippantly said something along the lines of 'It should have been out of the park'. We read this and thought, 'OK, let us see how well you hook because we are going to hammer your arse!' We really went after him in Perth. He scored ten and one.

That fourth Test match at Adelaide was one of the most satisfying wins of my career, to scrape home by one run. That really was a tremendous Test match, and if the Australians are fair-minded they will admit we should have won long before we did. Australia needed 186 to win when Kenny Benjamin had Langer lbw – they don't come any more plumb – but the umpire said 'not out'. When we saw the replay we wondered which way the umpire was looking. Langer top-scored with 54 and helped them get close. Tim May batted well for his 42 not out but we scampered home. Earlier in that match, I hit David Boon on the elbow and he reluctantly had to retire. That was a bit of a turning point as he was being quite stubborn until then. He never wanted to go off. As well as his mental toughness as a batter, he's a tough man physically. And you now know what happened at Perth, which had always been a happy hunting ground for West Indies. Even when we were hammered 5-1 in 1975–76 the one victory came at Perth. So heading to the WACA we knew they were going to lose – that was the way we felt.

I won the 1992 International Cricketer of the Year, which was nice recognition. Most of all I was pleased to contribute for my team with a record thirty-three wickets in the series, an improvement on my twenty-six in 1988–89.

Straight after this Australia tour we went to South Africa for a tri-series, along with Pakistan. We won that, too, so we were on a roll. Incidentally, on arriving back in the Caribbean at Barbados, there were a lot of board members there to welcome and congratulate us. I wasn't impressed and felt like asking them, 'Where were you when we flew out of the Caribbean?'

We left with no support, cleaned up in Australia and South Africa and all of a sudden we had lots of support again. We had to attend a celebration dinner, which was the last thing I wanted after being on the road for four months. I gave the officials attitude. I didn't like their double standards. We had to go up on stage and when they called my name I pulled my chair back in an intentionally noisy way that made me appear even angrier. I took my time to get up on stage, never smiled and generally did not appreciate the event. Tony Cozier wrote that I had an attitude issue and that my behaviour towards the officials was unbecoming. But nobody knew then why I was so annoyed. They do now.

We were on a high and supremely confident and believed that Pakistan had no chance when they arrived for our home series, even though we knew that we still had a job to do. We followed up with a 2-0 win against a competitive Pakistan team. We played some good cricket but the series ended in controversy at Antigua. Desmond Haynes was going for a third century in as many Tests and the umpires called the game off on the fifth morning with Desi 64 not out. The feeling was that Dickie Bird didn't really understand the Caribbean weather and he felt it was all over after an overnight downpour but within an hour or two the weather was good and the ground was dry; but, too late, the game had already been abandoned.

This series gave me my first proper look at a young Inzamam-ul-Haq and he scored his maiden Test century at the ARG. He loved to get on the front foot and was confident and was prepared to take you on and take up a challenge. He became even better over time; a very good player.

Later in the year I embarked on my first trip to Sri Lanka, which was very pleasant and we were well looked after. Unfortunately the scheduling was a bit of a joke as a one-off Test proves nothing. You have to have at least two Tests, but as it turned out we could not even complete the one game because of the weather.

It Was Caddick's Fault!

'I thought, "Ambi, you have messed up so you need to do something magical here." I was pumped up to make things right for my mistake'

It is interesting, maybe even funny, what motivates us sometimes. I was at my best when something was on the line, whether it was a match, a series or even my reputation. When England came to the Caribbean in 1994, we were already 2-0 up by the time we reached Trinidad but England showed some fight and were favourites to win when they required just 194 in their second innings. On this occasion, my reputation was on the line; if only in our own dressing room. This modest target was partly attributable to yours truly. When we batted second time around we were struggling for runs after England had managed a first innings lead of seventy-six. We were 227 for seven when I went in and joined Winston Benjamin. I remember the guys telling me on my way out, 'Ambi, you've got to bat long.' We were halfway through the fourth day so there was still plenty of cricket left. I was doing all right, had reached twelve and, when they took the second new ball, Andrew Caddick came on. Now, I don't know what it is about Caddick but every time he came on I just wanted to beat his bowling – I have no logical explanation why that was. It is not like we ever had words. If I had to give a reason for this irrational dislike of Caddick's bowling, I would probably say it was because he had an action quite similar to Sir Richard Hadlee's. I always admired Hadlee as a great cricketer and a truly great bowler and I figured, 'Man, you shouldn't be trying to bowl like Richard Hadlee, you know, you're not in the same class', so I wanted to show Caddick that he was no Hadlee and tried to beat his bowling.

In this particular innings I allowed my own feelings to get in the way of what the team needed from me, which was to bat time. Instead, I tried an ugly swipe through midwicket to a length ball and was bowled. I felt bad because I knew it was an irresponsible shot from a senior player. I was no batsman but I could handle a bat well enough and should have done better when my team needed more from me than that. I slowly strolled off and then sat in the dressing room thinking to myself, 'Man, you've really messed up here. You've let this Caddick thing get the better of you.' I was upset and so were the guys – they let me have it. It wasn't very often that I got an earful but this was one of those few occasions. They were not overly aggressive but they were not shy in expressing their disapproval either and said that I should have known better and that it was an irresponsible shot. I didn't respond because I knew they were right. I couldn't defend what was a terrible shot. I sat there a bit longer and after we were dismissed to leave England 194 to chase down, I thought, 'Ambi, you have messed up so you need to do something magical here.' I was pumped up to make things right for my mistake. By the time I walked on to the field to bowl, I was extremely focused and knew I could produce something that would prevent us from losing this game. Richie said to us before we went out to bowl, 'If we can take three or four wickets this evening we're in business' and would then be well placed for the final day. None of us expected the close of play score would be 40 for eight!

The innings could not have started any better with my old rival Mike Atherton gone to the very first delivery – leg before. It pitched on off stump and nipped back a bit. It was a good one for him to get first up. We always knew that Atherton was a big wicket as he was the captain and he could stick around and bat time if you don't get him early. In the same over England slipped to one for two when Mark Ramprakash was run out. He played me to long leg and tried to run a second to Courtney Walsh, who wasn't the best of fielders. The two was on but they were indecisive and it cost them. It was total madness on their part and I didn't quite understand what they were doing. Take the two or say 'no' – but to be run out first over was just stupid. I wouldn't say panic had set in at this point, though, as the pressure was still on us with England chasing a small target. They were two big early blows but I think the next wicket of Robin Smith was the moment where the tide turned as five for three was not a pretty scorecard for England and that really tilted the momentum. Smith tried to play forward to me and had his stumps knocked down. If you watch a replay of the shot front on it looks as though he played the perfect forward defensive, but from behind the stumps were scattered. He played it too late and was beaten for pace but I was bowling quickly that day. I added the wickets of Hick (caught behind) and Stewart – bowled when looking to punch down the ground – before Courtney had Ian Salisbury caught at slip. By that stage at 27 for six we knew it was game over and that there was no way they were coming back, but we wanted to win that evening and give ourselves a day off – but it wasn't to be. Not that we were disappointed because the captain had asked for 'three or four'. I watched the highlights later that evening in my hotel room and heard Michael Holding say after Stewart scored three off my bowling to put Hick on strike, 'Ambrose won't mind that too much' because he knew my record against Hick. And he was right!

I completed an incredible session by having Jack Russell caught at third slip and I then bowled Graham Thorpe, who played well in a stubborn way for his three (in forty-five minutes) before he got one that kept a bit low. The others were all decent deliveries. We got back into the dressing room on that fourth evening and some of the guys ribbed me by saying, 'Ambi man, we shouldn't be coming back tomorrow!' Courtney finished off the job nineteen minutes into the next day, removing Caddick and Chris Lewis. It was actually a decent Test match for England despite the end result, when they lost badly. I admired the way they showed some fight because they were 2-0 down and could easily have lost hope but they never did. We were always confident that we were going to win.

Alec Stewart recalled of one of England's lowest days: 'We turned up on that fourth day thinking we were going to win. We bowled them out just before tea and then it rained. So instead of West Indies having a two-hour session, they had an hour, which meant they would get one spell from Walsh and Ambrose, who were able to come steaming in and throw everything at us. Ambrose bowled "that" length that was too good for everyone. It was one of the most devastating spells of bowling that I've ever been involved with.'

Mike Atherton added: 'I had the feeling it would be a dangerous hour with how the game developed that day. We dropped a couple of catches we should have taken and ought to have been chasing no more than a hundred. That would have been a very different challenge. Instead we had Curtly and Courtney steaming in at us with nothing to lose. It was carnage.'

In terms of my overall great spells this performance is firmly in the top three because this spell swung the match our way. It also earned me a bonus of £50,000 from an English company, which had promised such a sum to the first West Indies bowler who claimed a ten-wicket haul in the series and the first batsman to score a century. We had agreed beforehand, though, that this money would be shared equally amongst the team.

So after three Tests the five-match series was all over. This was after we won at Jamaica and Guyana. The Sabina Park Test was significant personally because it was the first time that myself and the two Benjamins – all good friends from Antigua – had played in the same Test together. It was a special moment for all three of us. We had played together for the Leeward Islands but never West Indies. Graeme Hick played well for his 96 there because any player who scored runs against us well and truly earned them; we never gave anyone anything.

In Guyana, Richie won the toss and decided to bowl first to my amazement because it was a flat pitch and I felt we should make best use of it before it started to break up. Most of us weren't too happy and said words to the effect of 'Come on, skipper, in Guyana you win the toss and bat!' Richie was unmoved. We weren't happy but we supported him. When England slipped to two for two he probably felt as if he'd got it right until Mike Atherton and Robin Smith put on 171 and it looked like Richie's decision had backfired. But we won the game by an innings in the end and Richie had the last laugh. 'You see, guys, the skipper got it right!' he said with a smile.

In that game I bowled Atherton for a duck in the second innings to pick up my 200th Test wicket, which was a nice feeling even though I was never motivated by stats. What made it even better was that I was able to boast to my fellow Antiguan Andy Roberts that I had taken just forty-five Tests to take 200 Test wickets when it took him forty-six! I used to tease him about it and say, 'Well, this must mean that I am a greater bowler than you.' We'd laugh about it; it was all in good fun. What I do like about stats is the message it tells you about your bowling. For instance, I took twenty-five Tests to reach 100 Test wickets and only a further twenty to make it to 200, so it shows I was improving.

After going 3-0 up in Trinidad and moving on to Kensington Oval, Barbados – where we never lost – we started to think about another 5-0, like we used to see in the 1980s. The fighting England opener Alec Stewart had other ideas, as he scored two brilliant centuries. We felt there was no way England were coming back from 46 all out in Trinidad. Not only that, what made us even more confident of beating them was their eight-wicket defeat to a West Indies Cricket Board President's XI prior to the fourth Test. They were completely demoralised and seemed down and out. But this was Stewart's game and I always respected him for being a fighter. I realised it was going to take some work to get him out in Barbados so I tried to play on his patience because he got fed up if the boundary balls dried up. I started to bowl just wide of off stump and dry up the runs but he played very well and stuck around. It was a courageous and deserved win for England and I was impressed with the character they showed after they had been embarrassed by the Board XI in Grenada following a low day in Trinidad.

The fifth Test in Antigua was all about Brian Charles Lara and his Test record 375. Lara played so well that I didn't think they would ever dismiss him. He was in a bubble, a zone all of his own. The funny thing about this innings was the talk going on in the dressing room while Lara was despatching the England bowlers to all parts. Courtney was captain in the absence of the injured Richie Richardson and I said to him and a few of the other guys on the third morning, 'Gentlemen, we have won the series, we've batted for two days, Brian is [320 not out at the time] closing in on the world record, it's a very flat pitch so I suggest two things: let Brian smash the world record and score five hundred, and secondly, let's bat, bat and bat until they bowl us out – let's create some history and score a thousand!' I wouldn't say there was any laughter but my comments were greeted with surprise and some disapproval. But I was deadly serious. I recognised it was going to be difficult to bowl England out twice to win the Test match on that flat-ass surface so I thought it was time for records.

The former West Indies great Rohan Kanhai was the coach and he kept saying we had to try and win the game. I knew it wasn't going to happen. Courtney, under pressure from Kanhai, declared on 593 for five. I was upset. I said, 'Gentlemen, we cannot bowl them out twice on that pitch.' I thought they should at least have allowed Shivnarine Chanderpaul to score his maiden Test century as he was 75 not out and had scored a fifty in every Test since his debut in Guyana. I felt sorry for the youngster. Every break we had when we were in the field I let the guys have it, especially after Atherton and Smith had put on over 300. Even Chris Lewis hit 75 not out at number eight! I told them our declaration was nonsense. Maybe there was some kind of spiritual payback at play because when we were batting England took a *third* new ball, which is pretty much unheard of. Usually a team would take a second new ball and then the batting side is dismissed. But when Atherton claimed the third, myself and Kenny Benjamin were laughing wildly in the dressing room. We were howling, 'Boy, I've never seen any team take the third new ball. This is crazy, man!' But we had a dose of our own medicine as we too were taking a third new ball before too long. The match was drawn – surprise, surprise. But the series was comprehensively won 3-1.

Unbelievably, given how players are wrapped in cotton wool nowadays, I was flying to England to play a full season for Northamptonshire less than a week after this gruelling series. It should surprise no one, then, that I developed a bit of a niggle in my right shoulder during the course of that county summer. I have been blessed with superb natural fitness and have never had to do much gym work. In fact, the only time in my life when I did any gym was during that 1994–95 season, after I was advised to exercise the shoulder by a Jamaican specialist based in New York. He told me it was only wear and tear and that strengthening exercises would help me regain my fitness. The problem didn't stop me from bowling but I was unable to throw from the outfield. A London surgeon wanted to operate on it but the second opinion convinced me to just do some gym.

The downside to that injury was that it cost me a three-Test tour of India. I told the West Indies Cricket Board that India was a tough place to tour and that I had to be there. There was no Haynes and no Richardson so I wanted to help out Courtney, who was standing in as skipper, and add some experience, but the board insisted I stay back in the Caribbean to ensure I was 100 per cent fit for the Australia series at home. I never did get to play any Test cricket in India, which was a great shame. I was extremely disappointed but they were the bosses. We drew that series 1-1 and Courtney and Kenny Benjamin told me that if I had been there we would have won that series. Cameron Cuffy and Anderson Cummins never really turned up.

'Other than fast bowling, fitness was something else that came natural to Curtly,' said Desmond Haynes. 'You would never ask Curtly to go in the gym and lift weights and all that nonsense. But give him a ball and he would bowl a whole day for you. He confounds modern-day coaching trends where people talk up the gym culture to become a good bowler. From watching Curtly bowl

and other West Indian bowlers of that day, I came to believe in bowling fitness.
Curtly would practise on the flattest wicket with the most unhelpful ball and
groove his bowling until he had it down perfect.'

While the boys were in India, and with no cricket going on in Antigua at that time of year, I sharpened my fitness by playing football. I would train and play for West End Pressers with Winston Benjamin and it kept me fit. I really enjoyed it. They asked me to play for them the year before when they were in the First Division and I told them, in jest really, 'If you're promoted to the Premier Division, I will play.' So when they *were* promoted I felt like I should play, especially as there was no cricket. It wasn't without its hazards as so many players tried to take me out. They clearly figured, 'Who's this hotshot trying to play our sport?' But I could play – I just had to keep one eye looking out for those overphysical tackles. It was the same with basketball – everybody wanted to block Curtly Ambrose. I suppose it was an ego thing that some guys wanted to brag about. I had to bowl to be match fit for cricket but the football helped me to get physically fit. At the start of 1995 I knew cricket was coming up so I started to prepare myself. It never used to take me long to get into shape anyway because I have never carried excess weight. I can sit down and do nothing for a month and get up and start training again and I'm OK. Everyone's different. Courtney Walsh used to say if he sat around for two or three days he would feel sluggish when he started to train again. I'm lucky.

Before the Australians arrived, we had two Test matches to play in New Zealand, which was a useful series for me to try out the shoulder, though I felt 100 per cent fit by then. I had a taste of New Zealand at the 1992 World Cup. On this occasion I wasn't in the best of bowling shape. Physically I was fit but I hadn't bowled all that much since the end of the previous county season six months earlier. It's one thing running round the pitch and doing all the sprints but I needed more overs. I didn't bowl badly but I was overshadowed by Winston Benjamin, who scored 85 in the weather-affected first Test, and then Courtney, who bowled superbly well for his thirteen for 55 at Wellington in the second Test that we won easily. I remember the New Zealand coach saying after we racked up 660 for five declared – before his own team had batted – that it was a flat track and it would be a drawn game. That motivated us and put pressure on his batsmen, before we won heavily by an innings. It was a good warm-up for what was to come, especially with no Richie, no Desi and no Carl Hooper. We just started grooving nicely for the all-important series at home against Australia, when our world title was on the line.

'Curtly talks to no man!'

Michael Holding: Well, Curtly, you don't particularly like to give interviews. Why is that?

Curtly Ambrose: It's nothing that I've planned, it's just me. I just like to stay in the back seat and watch proceedings. I try as much as possible to stay away from interviews, cameras and stuff like that. Obviously when you're in the middle you can't get away from the public. After that I try to find myself somewhere quiet.

MH: But you must realise you're a star of the game and people want to know about Curtly Ambrose. How do you view that?

CA: Well, that is true, but it's not something that is in me. I feel very uncomfortable giving interviews and doing all the publicity stuff. It's not my style. That's why I try to stay away.

(Excerpt from a television interview with
ex-West Indies player turned pundit Michael Holding)

Over the years I have had a lot of guys approach me asking for an interview and sometimes I have given interviews but most of the time I haven't. Of course 'No' is always my first answer. But if they persevere a little maybe I will change my mind. But this reputation I developed for being unapproachable is so far from the truth because I am actually a down-to-earth, fun-loving kind of guy. But I accept my public reputation has been created from this serious game face I have worn for many years.

In the early part of my career I did agree to a few newspaper interviews – in the Caribbean and outside – and I found that they picked the quotes randomly and used whatever parts to tell the story they wanted to put out that may not have been an entirely true reflection of what I'd told them. Readers don't always get the whole story. I was concerned that the Curtly Ambrose the public was reading about was not exactly the Curtly Ambrose who gave the interview. So I figured early on, 'Let people judge me from what they see out on the cricket field.' I always preferred to do my talking with five and a half ounces in my hand, or a bat. I have never liked to talk about myself too much or wanted to be in front of the cameras too often. Others are happy with those things but it was never my style. Better that way than becoming annoyed with those guys putting my words down in a different way to how I said something. I am not anti-journalist or anti-media; I have nothing personal against them. That is just the way I felt while I was playing. I have since heard good explanations about how misrepresentation can occur, like if there is limited space in a newspaper to fit only half an interview into, but that really isn't my problem. I just want my words to be construed in the right way. I know most players don't mind the media stuff but I wasn't keen. That was just me. However, this tag I picked up, 'Curtly talks to no man!' – I have never said those words. That quote did not come from me and is a reputation the press gave me, but I understand why because I said very little to the media. I have since chilled out a lot on this over the years but that was my feeling towards the media when I was playing. My reluctance to agree to interviews had nothing to do with me not being comfortable speaking to the media. Speaking to someone is an easy thing to do. For me I just never cared much for talking about myself.

On a lighter note, I was reminded recently about how a *News of the World* reporter was chasing me for an interview in my heyday, unsuccessfully I should add. England were touring West Indies in 1990 when I found out that this reporter was trying to secure an interview with me through Viv Richards and I gave him short shrift. I asked him, 'Why are you speaking to Viv about interviewing me? You should come to me.' So he said, 'OK, Curtly, can I please interview you?' I replied, 'No!' At least I was consistent. I figured if you want an interview with me, come straight to the source, not a team-mate. Don't try to influence Viv, come to me. It sounds a little sneaky. To be fair to that reporter, though, I can understand why he did what he did because I was always looking kind of serious, especially when I was out there on the field. I have taken on commentary work since my retirement and I have become friends with some guys who told me that they used to be 'scared' to approach me for an interview because of this serious exterior I had so my reputation for shunning the media was a little intimidating. They figured I would embarrass them.

But when people get to know me they soon realise that I am not as fearsome as I appear to be.

I guess the way I acted with the media, reserved and stand-offish, was typical of my manner in general. I rarely said much to opposition teams either, though I would mingle occasionally with players I liked and respected. In the early stages of my career one of the customs at the end of every day was that the batting team would go into the dressing room of the team that had spent most of the day in the field and have a drink with them. Of course I have never drunk so that bit wasn't for me, but I would go over and say 'Hi' and chitchat a little. We wouldn't talk about the game too much. So this would go on in the early days of my career. But as schedules increased and games seemingly became more or over-competitive, that custom gradually disappeared. Players started to think, 'Boy, you beat up my bowling all day, I'm under a lot of pressure, I don't think I want to be laughing with you after the game.' It only ever really happened between West Indies, England and Australia. West Indians in those days all played county cricket and were familiar with that culture. By our 1995 series with Australia there was no more fraternising but there was a lot at stake and a fair bit of needle going on then.

Regarding Curtly's on-field and off-field manner, ex-England captain and old adversary Mike Atherton said: 'He was extremely quiet and never said anything on the field, certainly never sledged. He did his talking with the ball, though would occasionally stand and stare if the ball beat the bat. I can't remember one foul word coming out of Curtly's mouth; the same with Courtney Walsh

at the other end. I liked Curtly but didn't get to know him as a man, though I
respected him enormously as a bowler and enjoyed playing against him.'

In the days when we did mingle after play, I was, as I am now, the sort of person who is quite reserved, not shy, but if I don't know you I am not likely to start yapping away like some guys might do. But if someone comes over to say 'Hi' then I will talk. I will try to keep it short but I will talk. I am not going to embarrass anyone. There are two sides to Curtly Ambrose – highly competitive on the field but after play I am happy to say 'Hi' and be respectful to people. I don't normally take my work off the field. Over the years I have been closer to some of the English guys than anyone else because I have played county cricket with them and I feel comfortable with those guys. I've mentioned Lamby and David Capel at Northants, and Alec Stewart and Mike Atherton, too, as they are guys I have had battles with over the years and we will talk. I always gave Mike Atherton respect and would say, 'Morning, skipper', because being captain deserves respect. I would never say, 'Hi, Mike'. Even with Viv Richards nowadays I still call him 'Skipper'. Lamby is a bit different because we have shared a dressing room at Northants over the years so I would say, 'Lamby, what's up?' Ultimately, England is my second home after six years at Northants so I feel like I belong there. I can't say the same about Australia or New Zealand, although I got to know Stephen Fleming when he played for Northants' Second XI while I was there. When he started playing international cricket and then became captain I joked with him, 'You've come a long way, from that rookie I knew at Wantage Road!'

So there are guys I will have some banter with but I am generally reserved.

I have never been reserved amongst my own team, though. I contribute a lot in team meetings because I don't feel they should only be for the captain or the coach or senior players. I don't care how great you are as a cricketer, you don't know everything. That is impossible. So I believe contributions from everyone help. As great as some players are they will still miss things and need advice. It might take a junior player to point something out so that benefits the team better. We always had team meetings the night before the start of a match and on a rest day evening to ensure guys are switched on and focused to go again the next day. I was keen to contribute to these meetings as soon as I felt more comfortable in the dressing room and began to feel more confident expressing my opinions. I wanted to help in any way I could, in case some of the guys missed something. I know one or two things about cricket and my opinions have always been respected and valued whether as a player or, now, as a coach.

right: My father Joshua 'Jasper' Ambrose. He wasn't around much but we still loved him.

© *Curtly Ambrose*

above: My mother Hillie – the biggest influence on my life and especially my cricket.

© *Graham Morris/www.cricketpix.com*

above: Basketball with the boys – once my first love. © *Curtly Ambrose*

below: Lining up with the Swetes Village team (I'm on the end of the back row). © *Malverne Spencer*

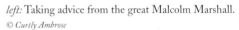

left: The scorecard shows I played for Swetes after West Indies were knocked out of the 1992 World Cup.
© *Malverne Spencer*

left: Taking advice from the great Malcolm Marshall.
© *Curtly Ambrose*

below: With my big buddy Courtney Walsh.
© *Graham Morris/www.cricketpix.com*

above: Celebrating a wicket on the 1988 England tour, Old Trafford. © *Bob Thomas/Getty Images*

above: In Barbados, where Rob Bailey was given out off my bowling. Replays showed it came off the thigh pad.
© *Graham Morris/www.cricketpix.com*

left: Another trophy – Leeward Islands won the Red Stripe Cup and the Geddes Grant Shield in 1994. © *Curtly Ambrose*

DOUBLE CHAMPION 1994 4 DAY + 1 DAY

above: Clip off the legs – batting in the 1990 NatWest Trophy, when we lost to Lancashire at Lords. © *David Munden/Popperfoto/Getty Images*

right: A proud moment, receiving the Order of Antigua & Barbuda. © *Curtly Ambrose*

Order of Antigua and Barbuda

Governor General Chancellor

To Curtly Elconn Lynwall Ambrose, Esquire

Greeting
The Award of the Order of Honour Silver Award in the Order of Antigua and Barbuda is hereby made to you and you are hereby authorized to have, hold, and enjoy the said Award, together with all and singular the privileges thereunto belonging or appertaining

Given under my hand and the Seal of the said Order this First day of November 1998

Instrument making the Award of the Order of Honour Silver Award in the Order of Antigua and Barbuda to Curtly Elconn Lynwall Ambrose, Esq.

above: Not my proudest day in cricket, as I clashed with Steve Waugh in the Trinidad Test, 1995. © *Allsport UK/ALLSPORT/Getty Images*

below: Debutant Matthew Elliott is caught behind in Brisbane, 1996. I always enjoyed bowling n Australia. © *Colorsport/REX*

above: Enjoying a rare smile with long-time rival Mike Atherton. © *Graham Morris/www.cricketpix.com*

below: What an honour – meeting the great man, Nelson Mandela, in February 1993.
© *Curtly Ambrose*

above: In my stride with my signature wristbands, at Lord's. © *Graham Morris/www.cricketpix.com*

above: Advising Reon King in England in 2000. I enjoyed my role as a mentor of the young fast bowlers. © *Graham Morris/ www.cricketpix.com*

left: Celebrating my 400th Test wicket at Headingley, 2000 – it was Mike Atherton! © *Graham Morris/www.cricketpix.com*

above: Receiving a guard of honour from England in my last Test… very humbling. © *Graham Morris/ www.cricketpix.com*

right: Bowling in my last Test series. © *EMPICS s8/n3/ Press Association Images*

left: Tall story! Playing
an exhibition game with
(my fellow 6ft 8in fast bowler,
Joel Garner in Grenada, 2008
© *Robert Hallan/REX*

below: Good rhythm is very
important for a fast bowler.
© *Graham Morris/www.cricketpix.com*

Antigua & Barbuda

To all and singular to whom these presents shall come, greetings.

Her Excellency Dame Louise Lake Tack GCMG, D.A.J

Governor General
Grand Master of the Order
Has invested and by these presents do invest

Curtly Elconn Lynwall Ambrose, Esquire

as a **Knight Commander** of

The Most Distinguished Order of the Nation
As witness by my sign manual. Given at Government House,
St. John's Antigua

This **Twenty eighth** day of **February**, 20 **14**

Valerie Smith
The Chancellor
Sealed and registered
No. **31**

Dame Louise Lake-Tack
Grand Master

right: The certificate for my Knighthood.

© Curtly Ambrose

below: Sir Curtly! Receiving my knighthood was a very proud day for the Ambrose family.

© Curtly Ambrose

left: White wedding! Me and Bridget were married in July, 2001. © *Curtly Ambrose*

below: Standing from left to right: Tanya, Shushanna, Beyoncé, Chloe, Latoya. Sitting: Bridget and yours truly © *Curtly Ambrose*

left: Here you see the routine for a touring cricketer, with all my luggage.

© *Graham Morris/ www.cricketpix.com*

right: Lazy Bass...I love playing music with my band

photo courtesy of www.spiritedband.com

above: Reaching 400 Test wickets – I would never have made it if it wasn't for the advice of my good friend Courtney Walsh to delay my retirement. © *Mirrorpix*

Waugh and Abdication

When [Steve Waugh] came back at me again with all guns blazing,
there was no holding back. I got seriously heated. I told him, 'Man, I
will knock you out – here and now. I don't care if I have no career left.'

West Indies' fifteen-year reign as the unofficial but widely acclaimed champions of world cricket was always going to end sometime. All cycles must come to an end and we had one hell of a ride as the best cricket team in the world. For us not to have lost a Test series in fifteen years was a quite incredible achievement, powered by many great players, unshakeable confidence throughout the team and a determination that whatever situation we might find ourselves in we would still come out triumphant. There were many times when we were challenged. Test cricket is not easy. In my time, from 1988, we came close to relinquishing our crown on several occasions, none more so than in my first series at home to Pakistan; but whenever we were taken to the edge, someone always produced the goods.

The 1995 home series against Australia was always going to

be a tough and demanding challenge as we had lost big-game players – legends, actually – and were striving to remain unbeaten without the likes of Richards, Greenidge, Marshall and Dujon; youngsters like Brian Lara and Shivnarine Chanderpaul were developing quickly, but we were not the force we had once been. That was clear. We were still a strong unit but not *as* strong. And while Australia had lost the great Allan Border a year prior to this clash, along with lesser but still good players such as Merv Hughes and Dean Jones, they were growing into a dominant force. Mark Taylor led a team which would go on to boast several all-time greats like Shane Warne, Glenn McGrath, Ian Healy, Steve Waugh, David Boon, Michael Slater, Mark Waugh, and more. It was only a matter of time before they leapfrogged us to become number one in the world.

The West Indies Cricket Board did the Aussies an almighty favour and ourselves a huge disadvantage when they ruled that Desmond Haynes, the elder statesman of our team, could not play in this four-Test rubber – purely because of a technicality. Desi was playing in South Africa with Western Province and, according to the WICB, you had to have been available for all five domestic first-class games in order to be eligible to make the Test team. Desi subsequently came back early from South Africa but missed the first game, playing for Barbados in the remaining four. He scored an unbeaten 201 against the Windward Islands and averaged 67 in his four games. Desi was thirty-nine at the time but was still the best opening batsman we had. Yet he wasn't selected because he missed that one game. My take is, yes, you have to have rules but when you have a player like Desmond Haynes there has to be some flexibility. It was clear he was trying to do the right thing by coming back early from Cape Town, but missed just one game. Haynes was a seasoned campaigner with fifteen years' Test experience; he was no rookie so deserved some flexibility. So we started that series with no Haynes and it turned out to be the end of his West Indies career. Stuart Williams and Sherwin Campbell were good players but at that stage they were rookies and it was unfair that they had to open up together against the might of Australia. Captain Richie Richardson eventually went up to open so it then left a gap in the middle order. Desi was the perfect man to guide Williams or Campbell.

That decision accelerated our decline and even now I am annoyed by the WICB's stance. It was nonsense and unnecessary and handed Australia a serious initiative that they would have been delighted about. This series ended 2-1 to Australia and Haynes might have made the difference in our favour. I am not saying we would have won or that it would have changed history in a long-term way. It was inevitable Australia were going to leapfrog us at some point with the talent they had, but it might not have started then.

Even without Haynes we still felt we would come out winners, despite the formidable challenge facing us. It was not to be, though. I admit I was not on top of my game and while I am not saying my performance had anything to do with our series loss, I knew that I wasn't firing like I could have.

We won the one-day series 4-1 so went into the Test series on a high. But that was soon shown to be of little relevance when Australia hammered us by ten wickets at the Kensington Oval, Barbados, to go 1-0 up. The big talking point from that match was a contested catch that Steve Waugh claimed off Brendan Julian to dismiss our star batsman Brian Lara, who was going well on 65 in our first innings. We never recovered from there. The whole team knew that it was not a clean catch and our suspicions were confirmed when the replay was shown, so we were all annoyed and unhappy. We thought it was not sportsmanlike of Steve Waugh to claim the catch. It is possible to take catches where you're not sure so you allow the umpires to decide. It never caused tension between the teams and we didn't give him any verbals thereafter as that was not really our style. That incident, once it was over, disappeared from our minds. The umpire was not going to change his mind so if you keep thinking about an incident that goes against you, you will lose focus. We just wanted to get him out because we knew how tough a cricketer he could be and how long he could bat; not for any other reason. Australia held on to that lead with two matches to go, following a draw in Antigua, where Richie wore a helmet for the first time in his career, something the Australians apparently viewed as a sign of weakness and vulnerability.

Brian Lara was the darling of Trinidad and, of course, when he was dismissed in controversial circumstances in Barbados the Trinidadians were not going to be happy. West Indians in general were not happy. So when we pitched up for the third Test in Port-of-Spain, the crowd were ready to show their feelings towards Steve Waugh. He would have known he was going to get some stick. You're always going to get some stick when you upset the local golden boy. As a team we had put it behind us but the crowd had not forgotten and I am positive that Steve Waugh would have endured some difficult times in the build-up to this match with the antipathy towards him after his 'catch that wasn't'.

The Trinidad pitch was juicy, quite green and had a lot of grass on it. It wasn't your typical Queen's Park Oval surface and therefore, unsurprisingly, it was a low-scoring game with neither team making more than 136. Plainly speaking, it was conducive to fast bowling. Steve Waugh made a gutsy 63 not out and showed that if you were prepared to battle it out you could score runs, though it wasn't an easy pitch to bat on. I enjoyed bowling on it and, even with my nine wickets in the match that helped us square the four-match series, I still was not at the top of my game. I was missing a bit of rhythm and wasn't feeling the ball out of my fingers as I should. I was still good enough to hold my own but knew I wasn't at my peak. The other fast bowlers could also sense that my rhythm was not quite there as on several occasions they wandered up to me and pointed out little technical issues like, 'You're falling away a little bit in your delivery stride.' They even offered to bowl some of my overs for me, but I was never one to shirk my duties. The media picked up on my struggles and some reporters suggested I was past my best. That was rubbish, though I was battling to find my best form.

That wasn't the only battle I faced in this match.

My pitch-side confrontation with Australia's number one warrior Steve Waugh in their first innings seems to have become infamous and it is something people ask me about all the time. But it is the only moment in my career that I experienced that kind of situation, because that is not part of my game. I've always respected Steve Waugh. He was a stubborn cricketer and a fighter. We had our battles and nothing was ever said between us on the field – until Port-of-Spain. This particular incident started while he was struggling to survive on a difficult wicket. He was really hanging on and playing and missing quite a lot. Even though he was fighting to stay at the crease for his country, there is no doubt he was struggling quite badly.

Anyone who has followed my career will be aware of my stare at batsmen. Some bowlers like to speak to batsmen and get involved in those sledging battles but I was happy with my stare. And when I got on top, my stare would last a little longer. It was my way of intimidating an opponent who was already hanging on just to remain there in the contest. I would add a bit more pressure. I didn't actually hear any cursing towards me coming from Steve Waugh's mouth. But when we went in for the break, Kenny Benjamin told me that he had cursed at me and had told me to 'eff off' and words to that effect. When I finish my stare at a batsman I turn round pretty quickly and therefore I didn't hear him. But the more I thought about what Kenny had said, the more I became heated inside. I thought, 'No, I can't allow this to just slide.' We had our battles previously but nothing was ever said so I thought this was disrespectful. He had scored runs against me in the past and I had never said anything. And here in Trinidad I was controlling the situation, had the better of him and he said this so I wasn't happy. I had always respected him and figured he respected me as well.

Confronting him in their dressing room was not my style. I was never going to do that, so when we got back out there after the break I had actually cooled down and thought, 'It's all right, just leave it, man.' In the heat of the battle things get said so I was prepared to leave it alone. But shortly after, I don't know what changed in my head but I suddenly snapped and I said to myself out loud, 'Man, I deserve a little more respect than this.' West Indies were under a lot of pressure at the time: 1-0 down in the series with our number one status on the line, there was pressure on me to deliver the goods with this being a pitch conducive to fast bowling and so, having reflected once again on what Kenny had told me, I approached Steve Waugh and asked him if he'd sworn at me. That's when he snapped back, 'I can say what I want to say', which was as good as admitting he'd sworn at me. That was when I ripped into him and let him have it: 'Man, don't you effing swear at me again.' And I don't swear a lot so for me to use expletives it was clear that my anger was at boiling point. I lost it. If he had said nothing to what I had asked him, or even told me he didn't swear, it would have ended right there, but when he came back at me again with all guns blazing, there was no holding back. I got seriously heated. I told him, 'Man, I will knock you out – here and now. I don't care if I have no career left.' That was when Richie intervened and told me to forget about it, and it was a good job he did because my ability to restrain myself was gone.

Richie was the leader so that was his job. He couldn't allow one of his players to get physical with the opposition so he did what he had to do. But I did want to get physical. I was going to beat him, I was that mad. I certainly was not worried about any ban or anything like that at the time. Beating him would have given me some satisfaction. Quite simply, I never expected that from him. If it had been the first time I had played against him and didn't know him I could maybe have accepted it because I would have figured 'This guy needs to be shown that you don't speak to Curtly Ambrose like that' and then let my five and a half ounces do my talking. But this was the fourth Test series that Steve Waugh and I had played against one another. After I walked away I had still not calmed down and I remained furious for some time.

Inevitably the next ball was a bouncer and he just about got out of the way – and the crowd loved that because these Trinidad supporters had still not forgiven Steve Waugh for claiming that dubious catch off Lara in Barbados. I started bowling quicker and had Waugh jumping and hopping all over the place. By now I stopped thinking about the physical part of it and began to think like a fast bowler again but I still wanted to make life extremely uncomfortable for Waugh. In reality I never actually wanted to hurt Steve, but in the heat of battle I was trying to make things difficult for him and therefore I lost my cool. I wanted to make things as hard and uncomfortable as possible for him. I was really heated and the crowd were with me all the way.

Gradually I calmed down and told myself, 'Come on now, you're a professional and you're better than this. Focus on the job at hand.' Of course that was to bowl Australia out rather than trying to target Steve Waugh. If you watch the footage you will see that I was smiling again before long so all the nastiness happened in the heat of the moment but was over with pretty quickly. I lost it for a moment but soon realised after going back to my fielding position that batsmen had rattled or frustrated me before like Javed Miandad, David Boon, Jack Russell and others, yet I had always managed to stay calm and deal with the situation in my own way – with the batsman not quite knowing what I was thinking. This incident with Steve Waugh was not my way but I can't change history. It happened and I am not proud of it. He ended up being not out but I wouldn't say he won because I gave him a torrid time. In fact my first priority during that particular spell wasn't getting him out; it was to make life extremely difficult for him, which was my way of saying, 'You had better think twice before you try to rattle me again!'

We were reported to the match referee, Majid Khan, who reminded us that we're all professionals and this kind of incident does not look good for the game, and that two seasoned campaigners like us should know better than to act in this manner. He spoke to us in a very understanding and professional way and asked us to refrain from this kind of behaviour. I honestly thought both of us would have been fined – at least some percentage of our match fee. It was not good for cricket and we were both very lucky to get off with no action taken against us. It was unbecoming conduct for sure and I never usually played my cricket like that so I would not have complained had I been punished. It was the only time I was involved in such a confrontation. Steve Waugh and I have never talked about it – ever. It started right there on the pitch and ended right there on the pitch. I have lost count of the number of times people have asked me about it and I just dismiss it as one of those things in cricket. I never talk about it and I don't think he does either. It is the hype over the years which has made this legendary. I try to deal with it light-heartedly as it's done and dusted. I was asked about it at a speaking event in Australia a few years ago and I explained that Steve 'politely and respectfully asked me to . . . eff off!' They enjoyed that. Seriously though, the good thing is I never lost any respect for him and I don't think he lost any respect for me. It was something that happened between two tough competitors who wanted to win.

So we headed to Jamaica level at 1-1 and also loaded with confidence after our win in Trinidad. Who would have thought, then, we would lose this match at Sabina Park by an innings and with it give up our world crown? We won the toss and scored 265, before Australia's 531. I don't agree with those who suggested we should have put them in because we bowled them out for 128 and 105 in Trinidad. Teams at this level are professional and the last game should not matter. The biggest example is England a year earlier. We bowled them out for 46 and then in the next Test they beat us badly in Barbados. We thought it was a good pitch to bat on but we just didn't make best use of it. And, of course, during their innings the Waugh brothers piled on the runs as Mark hit 126 and Steve 200, after he was dropped on 42 by debutant wicketkeeper Courtney Browne off Kenny Benjamin.

Courtney Browne has always carried the can for that defeat for dropping Steve Waugh, but I and many of the guys felt more anger towards Junior Murray, the man he replaced. Murray dropped out of the team two days before the match – with a severe headache. He had two days to recover and we all felt it was a weak excuse and that he could have played the game. It wasn't like he had a broken finger or anything like that. He said he knew his body and he wouldn't be ready in time. We felt he should have tried harder to be ready and were disappointed. What made Murray's absence worse was *that* drop by Courtney off Steve Waugh. That changed the whole game, though I am not going to say that lost us the game and the series, because one drop cannot lose you a game. I actually felt sorry for Courtney that he was put in that position.

After the defeat we became even angrier with Junior Murray because if he was playing he would probably have taken what was a routine catch to dismiss Steve Waugh. It might then have been a different game. This wasn't any average match for him to skip; there was a series on the line and our prestige after fifteen years of dominance. We still remind Junior of how we thought he chickened out on us when we get together all these years later. We laugh about it now but back then it was no laughing matter. We told him at the time he was weak-hearted. We're not the type of people to hold it against him moving forwards and that is why he played in the first four of those five Tests on the 1995 tour of England, because we would rather pick our best team all the time. But after that game in Jamaica I was still angry with Murray and said to Richie Richardson and the guys, 'Let's not take him to England, let's leave him in the Caribbean. We have Courtney Browne, and Ridley Jacobs is doing well for Leeward Islands. I can't go into battle with a man who is willing to give up without trying.' I have seen Jeffrey Dujon play with broken fingers, so having discovered that Junior Murray was not prepared to fight with his team-mates in a crucial match made me feel that I didn't want him in my team. I want to be able to count on my team-mates when times are tough. My opinion was listened to but ultimately ignored as the selectors went back to Junior for England. I can safely say, though, that if Viv Richards had been captain he wouldn't have been on the tour. Viv would not want anyone in his team who was not prepared to fight. Either that or he would have been forced to play with his headache and prepared to fight to the end. Richie was a bit more forgiving.

It was a very sombre dressing room after we lost that series. It was our first series loss to Australia in nineteen years as well so we not only gave up our number one status but the Frank Worrell Trophy also. We felt grossly disappointed and nothing much was said. Everyone was saddened as a lot had gone down the drain – being undefeated in a series for fifteen years was a record we did not want to give up. I felt we had destroyed a legacy. This was the first time I had lost a series so it was painful. I had seven years of winning; Courtney and Richie were closer to a decade. The younger guys would not have felt the pain quite so much because they never knew what it was like to be number one for such a long time. We had grown up in the team with the likes of Greenidge, Haynes, Richards and Marshall and the pride in winning was instilled in us. We tried to pass that feeling down to the rookies who came in after us. It was inevitable our run would end at some point, but I never thought our decline would continue for so long. I am a realist and knew there would come a time when we would drop in the rankings because when you lose great players it takes time for youngsters to develop.

When we were the best team in the world for so long nothing was ever done to nurture the talent that we had coming up. The WICB and other territorial boards were complacent and just sat back and believed we would always be top because we had talent. While this complacency was going on, Australia were setting up academies and building from grass roots for the future. England followed suit years later. Our cricket has sometimes been a shambles since we lost our number one status and these aspects have been a factor. When Australia lost McGrath, Warne, Gilchrist and the rest they went through a short period when they struggled but their decline lasted maybe two or three years. The fact West Indies' decline has lasted for almost twenty years is a hard pill to swallow.

As for Australia, the new Kings of Cricket, they had talent and good leadership bursting at the seams. Mark Taylor led them in this series and he was another of those guys, like Graham Gooch and David Boon, who was not especially attractive as a batsman but he got the job done. He was a fighter and a decent player – but more, a great leader. I respected his leadership qualities, while he had safe hands at slip. His cool exterior was perhaps his most impressive asset. We had some battles and he never looked ruffled, always appeared cool and calm. Even if he was under pressure as skipper he never showed it. Maybe back in the changing room he would let the guys have it, I don't know. But from what I saw he never looked flustered and seemed to be in control all the time. Taylor followed a great leader in Allan Border and was succeeded by another in Steve Waugh. It was an embarrassment of riches in terms of gutsy leadership, with all three being excellent batsmen. I have seen them all and it's touch and go for me as to who was the best captain, purely from an opponent's view, between Border and Taylor – no disrespect to Steve Waugh. The reason I would give Allan Border the edge is because he inherited a weak Australia team and moulded an average side into a great one. When he left, Mark Taylor took over and continued that trend – while the West Indies struggled to catch up.

Trouble in the Ranks

'I chastised Lara about his attitude and about him not giving 100 per cent to the team and I started to swear and when I do that the guys know I have really had enough. I told him that he was a professional and he should behave like a professional'

We were now seeking to rebound from the rarity of a series loss, to Australia, though we were still confident of winning in England. There was just one problem. It turned out to be the most challenging and difficult tour I have ever been on in my entire career, especially in reference to the ridiculously long schedule.

Our first game was 13 May and the last on 3 September 1995 after two games against Yorkshire at Scarborough – this after a six-Test series! Can you imagine how I felt after a long, tough series to be told we then had to go and play some cricket at Scarborough? That itinerary was so bad we even played Somerset in not one but *two* three-day games at Taunton, where Jimmy Adams got hit quite badly by an Andre van

Troost bouncer. Although he was very quick I am sure it happened because of exhaustion. And we had as many as five games between the third and fourth Tests, including fixtures against Ireland, the Minor Counties and Sir J.P. Getty's XI. It was a long, long, tiring tour for us and we were burned out. The schedule killed us and undoubtedly had an impact on our performances in the Test series. I don't know how the WICB agreed to that itinerary. I believe the schedule was designed by the English board to burn us out and it worked, but the WICB should never have agreed to it. We were dead beat on this tour after a tough series in the Caribbean against Australia.

The other challenging part of this trip centred on team disunity or, more to the point, Brian Lara's conduct that was unattractive for a top international cricketer. We had some issues with the great Brian Lara starting back in the Caribbean in the Australia series. Actually, the problems were more between Brian and the captain Richie Richardson. A lot of people thought Brian wanted his job. I wasn't sure but I sensed that Brian did not support Richie to the fullest. These issues that were hovering about the team became clearer in a meeting after the Jamaica Test against Australia, prior to going to England. Brian said he wasn't in the mood to go to England and, again, it was my view that this was borne out of his feelings about Richie's captaincy. So even though Brian did eventually tour there was friction and still some problems going on.

This ongoing problem came to a head when Brian left the tour between the fourth Test in Manchester and the fifth in Nottingham. Richie is a laid-back guy and he can put up with a lot before he snaps but there came a point when he could not take any more with Brian. We had a team meeting in Taunton before the second three-day match against Somerset and he really chastised Brian for being 'egotistical'. It was nothing to do with Brian's batting – after all he had just smashed 87 and 145 at Old Trafford. But Richie felt Brian was undermining his leadership. Richie said he couldn't deal with egotistical people and Brian really took it personally and said a few things back and walked out of the meeting. We didn't know where he went but we learned that he had left the tour. He was AWOL for a few days.

Discussions between Brian, the tour management and the WICB president Peter Short saw Brian return to the squad in time for the next match against Gloucestershire at Bristol. I wouldn't want to speculate on the nature of those discussions but when the news came from the manager Wes Hall that Brian would be rejoining the team, most of the guys were not too happy, including me. We knew he was a great player and would make a significant difference to the team, but the manner of his walkout was grossly disrespectful to the captain and the team. I asked the manager, before Brian returned, whether he thought Brian would act differently when he came back. The manager's answer was 'I don't think so'. I felt that he should not have been allowed to come back and the officials could have dealt with it at the end of the tour, back in the Caribbean. It seemed to me that in some people's eyes Brian Lara was bigger than the team.

This was another example of West Indies Cricket Board insularity and politics where decisions are made not on merit but on the strength of a guy's reputation or the island where he comes from. I have seen it many times where guys have erred in far less a way and have been treated harshly, when maybe only a slight reprimand was required. For instance, Winston Benjamin was sent home from this tour for, in my view, doing nothing wrong. He was extremely ill and was not able to play the game against The Universities at The Parks, when they wanted him to play. His condition improved slightly during the game and he tried casually kicking a football with the guys before the game, and it didn't go down well with management. Their take was 'You are too ill to play the game but you can play football . . .?' They sent him home on disciplinary grounds, presumably after consulting with the WICB. That cost him not only the remainder of that tour but his international career. I also heard that some WICB officials wanted to ban Kenny Benjamin for life because of not wearing his blazer on this tour, even though there was a perfectly good reason for this. So the Brian Lara episode shows how inconsistently cricket in the West Indies can be managed.

I do not believe the fact the two Benjamins were both from Antigua is mere coincidence. I come back to the insularity and political bias of our cricket once more. When you're from the Leeward Islands, or Windward Islands, you are not treated the same way as players from the larger territories like Guyana, Trinidad, Jamaica and Barbados. The facts are there. It has been a trend for many years. Some esteemed cricket visionaries down the years, such as the late, great Sir Frank Worrell, who was one of the more outspoken against West Indies' insularity, have said that the future strength of West Indies cricket is dependent on the development of the smaller islands. This should be a pointer towards the WICB becoming more all-encompassing and welcoming of players outside the Big Four. I am not pointedly criticising the current regime, as this is a culture that has existed for many, many years. But the present incumbents do have the chance to put things right for the good of West Indies cricket, by giving more influence and opportunity to the smaller islands.

Going back to the Lara episode, I am not going to say I have always been a saint. But whatever I have said that may have upset people has always been in the best interests of the team. I have become heated and aggressive in team meetings but have never walked out because it is about honesty and what is best for the team. For Brian to have been invited back was hurtful because it suggested he *was* bigger than the team. This is not personal against Brian Lara because we have always got along fine; I am speaking generally. If I had acted in the way that Brian had I would have expected to have been kicked off the tour and dealt with accordingly.

This unpleasant incident left a very bitter taste in my mouth and, as is typical of the passionate and honest way that I react at moments like these, I told the coach Andy Roberts and manager Wes Hall that at the end of the tour I would no longer play for the West Indies. I told them that I would continue to play county cricket or seek a contract in South Africa or Australia. This decision had nothing to do with my cricket; it centred on how the WICB seemingly had a higher regard for one man than the team. I was a big player in the team as well and had never acted in that way, no matter how upset I might have been or how much I spoke out in team meetings or even cursed at times. I was not impressed, which is why I told Andy and Wes that I was out of there. They tried to talk me out of it throughout the fifth Test at Trent Bridge, which I missed with injury. They worked on me for several days. I deferred judgement then but finally decided, after thinking about it further at home, that it was not the right time for me or West Indies cricket to bow out then. As angry as I was about the whole thing, I felt that I should not allow the Brian Lara saga to end my career. I always said I would end my career when I wanted to end it.

> West Indies legend Andy Roberts, coach on that tour, recalled: 'When Curtly told me he was retiring I thought he was joking. He had far too much cricket left in him. Even when he finally retired in 2000, I still thought he could have played on for another three years.'

This series, despite all the off-field politics, actually started well with a comprehensive win at Headingley. England pulled it back to 1-1 at Lord's, thanks to Dominic Cork's seven for 43 in the second innings on his debut. Then we turned up for the third Test at Edgbaston and were greeted by a pitch that I can only describe as peculiar. When we saw the pitch for the first time it looked terrible; that is putting it mildly. Both ends were shaved of grass and were just dry. But in the middle there was green grass. I thought it was a strange-looking, terrible pitch and I didn't know what to make of it. England captain Mike Atherton won the toss and decided to bat. As we were going out I said to the guys, 'This pitch looks like it could be flat but the first ball I'm going to bowl will be a bouncer to see what kind of response we get.' So when the bouncer took off and flew high over Junior Murray's head for four wides, I thought, 'Wow, this is going to be trouble', and a bit different from what I had expected. I felt they had tried to limit the threat of our fast bowlers by shaving the grass from the two ends but had neglected to think about our bouncers from the middle of the pitch. After I sent Atherton and Thorpe back to the pavilion (at 53 for three), I told the guys this pitch would backfire on England and that I would take ten in the match. However, it wasn't to be. I pulled up after 7.5 overs with a pain in my inner thigh. I would happily have gone through the pain barrier but I couldn't even run in; I could hardly walk. I was cooked and that was my Test done. I batted a little but never bowled another delivery. It was a shame from a personal viewpoint as I fancied getting among the wickets, but the guys got the job done without me quite comfortably and we won by an innings to go 2-1 up.

England came back to 2-2 at Manchester and although the scores and the eventual six-wicket win suggest it was a comfortable victory, we should actually have gone 3-1 up even though England needed just 94 to win. We made some blunders and they cost us. They were 48 for four which was effectively 48 for five with Robin Smith retired hurt because of a broken cheekbone after he was hit by an Ian Bishop bouncer. There was a point when Richie made some questionable bowling changes. He took off Kenny Benjamin and brought me back, to the amazement of Kenny and most of us as he was into a real good spell and had picked up a couple of wickets. England were on the ropes. I wasn't bowling well. It could have been a much closer game.

After Brian Lara rejoined the squad for the fifth Test, following his brief exit from the tour, we had what was supposed to be a tactics meeting before the Trent Bridge Test. But I was very upset with Brian and had to say something; that meant this would not be your average team meeting but would be quite an explosive team talk. The way I usually express my grievances in team meetings is to criticise collectively, as it is about the team rather than individuals. But when I am especially unhappy I will start calling names. And in this meeting I called out the captain Richie Richardson and told him what I thought of his batting, then I called Jimmy Adams and told him the same, and again with Carl Hooper. My concerns were about the senior batsmen stepping up and raising their game.

I purposely left Brian Lara's name until last. It was difficult to criticise his batting after his 87 and 145 in a losing cause in Manchester. But I chastised him for his attitude and about him not giving 100 per cent to the team and I started to swear. When I do that the guys know I have really had enough. I told him that he was a professional and he should behave like a professional. I said, 'When you want to score runs you will score runs; these England bowlers cannot get you out when you are focused.' I chastised him severely because I knew he had more to offer than the other batsmen. I suppose it was a back-handed compliment because I knew what he was capable of. Brian did not respond or try to state his case because he had known me a long time and one thing the guys will tell you is that I am fair. I mark myself as hard as I mark my team-mates. I will give you a chance. Brian seemed to heed my advice and batted magnificently as he went on to score 152, 20 and 179. I was forced to miss the fifth Test through injury. There, we saw England's spinners, Mike Watkinson and Richard Illingworth, give us some problems, so we expected our leg-spinner Rajindra Dhanraj to bowl them out. We felt he was better than both of their guys, but he didn't perform and that cost us. We had to settle for a draw, as we did in the sixth and final Test, so 2-2 it finished, as was the case on the '91 tour also.

There were disciplinary issues all through that England tour. At the end of the series, back home in the Caribbean, Brian Lara, Carl Hooper, Kenny Benjamin and myself had to face a disciplinary committee in Barbados, all for different reasons: Brian Lara for his walkout; Carl Hooper for not turning up at Scarborough for those last two games of the tour; Kenny Benjamin for the West Indies blazer issue, and for me it was quite similar. Kenny was never actually given a blazer that fitted him throughout the tour and was often using borrowed ones that didn't fit right either, despite him complaining about it almost every day. In my case, we were asked to wear a West Indies blazer back home on the plane though when Wes Hall called everyone in their room the night before we flew, to advise about the dress code, I was not there and never got the message.

Apparently the original plan for every player to fly back to his own island had changed and we were all now flying back to Barbados together before going our separate ways. I never got to hear any of this and when I came down into the hotel lobby on the morning of our departure I saw all the guys in their blazers. I was in my denims. The first I knew of our uniform request was when Richie asked me where my blazer was, while we were boarding the bus. Then the manager suggested I got changed before we flew but I reasoned that my blazer and shirt were creased and crumpled in my bag and even if I put them on I would look more of a mess. I did check on the condition of my blazer in my suitcase when we reached the airport but it wasn't in a good state. Not only that I would have looked foolish wearing my blazer with jean pants and a denim shirt. I preferred to be the odd man out than to look stupid. I wore my West Indies blazer with pride normally but in this case it wasn't right. When we reached the other end and were met by flashing cameras it didn't look good for me. But Wes Hall did state in his end of tour report that I was the only one who did not receive his message. After Brian and Carl Hooper had their hearing in the morning, I had a hearing later with Kenny. I explained my case but they still fined me – all four of us, actually – 10 per cent of my tour fee. It was a tough tour yet here I was handing some of my hard-earned salary back to the WICB for, effectively, not being in my hotel room to pick up a message from the manager!

The only other occasion I was disciplined in my career was for smashing down my stumps after we had lost the Barbados Test to England in 1994. I was bowled by Chris Lewis to end the game and I then knocked the one remaining stump out of the ground. There were dozens of spectators running on the pitch, it was game over, I was disappointed about losing the match and I knocked one stump over. The ICC match referee, John Reid, fined me $1,500 and justified it with a crappy reason. He told me that many times when I was dismissed I had 'threatened' to knock the stumps out the ground. How can you punish someone for something they 'almost' did over several years? If I wanted to hit stumps I wouldn't have missed. It was just a habit. I reluctantly accepted my fine but I wasn't happy at all, as it was a black mark against my name. I was very upset about it. We had the hearing in Antigua before the fifth Test and I thought, 'I'm on home territory, he's being harsh, shall I just rough him up?' Ultimately I figured he wasn't worth the trouble but I honestly felt like roughing him up. It's incredible to think that I was fined $1,500 for something pathetic like that and when I'd almost punched Steve Waugh in the middle of a Test match I got away with a warning. Not the most consistent of punishments.

World Cup Chaos

'We started to feel like it was our World Cup once we reached the semi-finals'

The 1996 World Cup should have had West Indies' name inscribed on the trophy – and would have had we not blown our golden opportunity in the semi-final in a crazy spell of cricket that still haunts me to this day. That World Cup remains a frustration and a disappointment to me because I wanted to win a World Cup medal and never did. In my other two World Cups, 1992 and 1999, we were never in them and were eliminated early so we had no chance. But in '96 we should have won. A World Cup win would have been the icing on the cake in my career. I realise most one-day internationals are rarely remembered but World Cups are a big deal.

The campaign, even from our preparations, did not go to plan initially when our star batsman, Brian Lara, missed the tri-series in Australia for personal reasons. It always provides an opportunity for another batsman, but you just cannot replace a batsman as good as Brian. Fortunately he was back with us in time for the World Cup in India, Pakistan and Sri Lanka. Incidentally, Brian's absence on that Australia tour meant that I almost had my first taste of captaincy of the West Indies team but the reason it didn't happen is quite simple: I didn't want it. I have never seen myself as a captain, it's not for me; even as far back as when I was playing for Swetes. Being a premier fast bowler is hard enough work and I always believed that I could lead from the front with a ball in my hand. I tried to be a leader without having the title of captain. This opportunity was offered me in January 1996 when we had a fifty-over game against Australia A. Richie injured his hamstring while batting in the first innings and, with no Courtney Walsh playing either, I was asked to lead the team in the field as the next senior player. I respectfully refused so Phil Simmons captained. I didn't have to think about it; I told them straight away. The coach, Andy Roberts, and Richie didn't hold it against me and nothing changed. But they did seem surprised when I turned it down and asked, 'Why?' That's just me.

With Brian back in the ranks, our World Cup campaign started with a victory against Zimbabwe, a game we were expected to win, of course. Nothing was straightforward in that tournament for us, though, as we then lost our next three games against India, Sri Lanka and, embarrassingly, Kenya. We didn't bat particularly well against India but had them on the ropes for a brief period, while they chased 170-odd. Unfortunately Courtney Browne dropped Sachin Tendulkar early off Ian Bishop, as he ran round to square leg, and India won the game. Poor Courtney: first Steve Waugh, then Sachin!

We forfeited the Sri Lanka match, like Australia, as we didn't feel safe going there at a time when there was some unrest in the country. We didn't want to play under duress. It was a unanimous decision after looking at all the pros and cons, assessing the points we could take from upcoming matches. Ultimately, though, it was about our safety.

Some people suggested our decision not to go to Sri Lanka backfired on us when we lost to Kenya but I didn't agree; that decision was purely made on safety grounds and had nothing to do with the cricket. The Kenya game was, quite simply, a total disaster. We chased 167 and were 93 all out. Kenya were fresh on the scene and nobody gave them a chance of beating us. They should never have scored that much in the first place but we should still have won that game easily. It's not easy to excuse this defeat and I would not want to do so because it was unforgivable. But some things went on that did not help matters. For instance, Carl Hooper pulled out of the squad for family reasons just before the World Cup; to lose his world-class batting and useful off-breaks was a huge blow. We all felt the obvious replacement would be Phil Simmons, who wasn't in the original squad. The selectors, though, replaced Carl with Cameron Cuffy, a decision I still cannot fathom to this day. We didn't need another fast bowler in the subcontinent with myself, Bishop and Walsh. However, as peculiar as that selection was, the Kenya result was unacceptable and it hurt. I had a reputation for speaking my mind in the dressing room and, as I have made clear, wasn't afraid to let players know if I felt they were not doing their jobs. But on this occasion I packed my kit and left, saying nothing. No one could explain this result to me in a way that would make any sense.

We met Australia next, knowing we had to win if we wanted to stay in the World Cup. We were still hurting from the Kenya match so the guys were out to right a few wrongs. We were really fired up. Richie played extremely well and saw us through with 93 not out. Then it was South Africa in the quarter-finals. They were unbeaten up to that point after winning all of their five group matches. They provided a stern challenge, but Brian Lara scored a brilliant hundred (111 off ninety-four balls) and after this result we started to feel like we were invincible, having come through tough challenges against Australia and South Africa. It's amazing how quickly you can put a result like the Kenya one behind you once you revert to winning ways against top sides.

We went into that semi-final against Australia in Mohali brimming with confidence. The Kenya humiliation was far from our minds and instead we knew that we had already beaten the Aussies in the group stage so there were no issues as far as self-belief went. Both teams were stuffed with big-game players: in the yellow corner there were the likes of Mark and Steve Waugh, Shane Warne, Glenn McGrath and the great one-day batsman, Michael Bevan. In the red corner there was Ambrose, Walsh and Bishop with the youthful magic of Brian Lara and experience and quality of our skipper, Richie Richardson. I would say the teams were quite evenly matched. It had not been a year since Australia had stolen our Test world champions crown from us so we both had a fair claim to the favourites tag. The mood in our dressing room could not have been better in the build-up to this match. We started to feel like it was our World Cup once we reached the semis. I don't say this to give the impression we were complacent; just supremely confident.

That buoyant mood immediately translated into our cricket, even though we lost the toss and were asked to bowl first. We had Australia on the ropes at 15 for four after myself and Ian Bishop had taken two apiece. I had taken the danger man, Mark Waugh, in the first over of the match before Bish snapped up their skipper, Mark Taylor. It was soon eight for three when I trapped Ricky Ponting lbw. Bish completed an incredible spell by bowling Steve Waugh. We were cock-a-hoop and figured that was it and that we would go on to finish the game off. But Bevan and Stuart Law shared a big partnership (138) that gave them a fighting chance. The frustration was that Roger Harper, normally a great fielder, dropped Law at short midwicket early in his innings and then Courtney Browne – again – missed a stumping off Harper that would have got rid of Bevan. So we had ourselves to blame that Australia managed to scrap their way to 207 for eight off their fifty overs. Still, it was a total that we should have chased down and we were pretty confident.

Chanderpaul batted well for his 80 but he gave it away when we were 165 for two with nine overs remaining. He later claimed he was tired and cramped up and tried to hit out and got caught at mid-off. We said to him, well, if you're struggling, why did you not just keep the singles ticking over and get down to the other end to catch your breath? He was inexperienced, though, at twenty-one, so we kind of forgave him. His wicket really did change the game as we were coasting to victory only to slip to 202 all out in the last over. It didn't help that we were up against one of the best bowlers of all time with leg-spinning genius Shane Warne bowling an especially miserly spell (three for six in three overs). But we made some poor decisions and with Richie Richardson out in the middle batting very well, the coach, Andy Roberts, took control of the batting order – and panicked. He promoted big-hitters Roger Harper and Ottis Gibson to try and hit us over the line and they went up the order ahead of Jimmy Adams and Keith Arthurton, which to me was ridiculous. We were not struggling; we basically needed a run a ball but for some reason we suddenly acted like frightened rabbits caught in the headlights. It wasn't like we needed fifteen an over and required power hitters. Richie was playing really well and, with Jimmy or Keith Arthurton, would have found the gaps to have got us over the line for sure.

Those poor decisions cost us and it was the end of our World Cup. I went in at number ten when we needed six runs but got run out after calling Richie through for a bye. We stood there for five or ten minutes waiting to hear my fate. I told Richie I was safe so was surprised when the Pakistani third umpire Khizer Hayat gave me out. I would never have been out there if we had kept our composure as we would have won the game at a stroll. There is no way that Sri Lanka would have beaten us in the final like they did the Aussies – no way. By that stage we were so confident and were playing some really good cricket, which will puzzle some considering that disastrous result we had against Kenya. In the aftermath of that Australia loss, we were packing our kit away when Richie gestured to me to come and sit next to him in the dressing room. He told me he was done with cricket and was going to retire. I tried to convince him to stay on and not feel pressured to stand down in the heat of the moment. But he felt he wasn't getting enough support as captain. Richie was only thirty-four at the time and he was leading the side well enough, was still batting well and I felt he had more cricket in him. He wasn't the aggressive leader that Viv was but was good in his own quiet way. Richie had already sent his resignation letter to the WICB by then so it was clear that he had made up his mind. I was disappointed as a team-mate, as a friend and as a fellow Antiguan. It was just another reason to feel sad about a tournament that should have ended in far happier circumstances, for Richie and the West Indies.

Less than a fortnight after our heart-wrenching defeat in the World Cup, we were facing New Zealand in the West Indies, for five ODIs and two Tests. In that short time there was a key development, namely the announcement of Richie's successor. Brian Lara made no secret that he wanted the captaincy, even while Richie had the job, and I thought he was a bit hasty in making his ambitions known so publicly. It was obvious he was going to captain West Indies eventually because he was much younger than Courtney Walsh. The likely scenario appeared to be that Courtney would lead the team for a couple of years and then Lara would take over. There was no question about it and that is what happened. Lara was too anxious to lead the West Indies and should have bided his time and waited his turn. I was not too happy that Brian expressed his captaincy ambitions in the media as he did. I felt that it did not send a good signal. The Jamaicans were not too happy with Brian, naturally, as they were on Courtney Walsh's side and therefore did not appreciate how Walsh was challenged by Lara for the captaincy. Almost inevitably, the first ODI of the tour was in Jamaica and the locals started to speak out quite aggressively towards Lara, who they figured had disrespected Courtney.

There was tension in the air as a few threats had been made against Brian. Jamaicans are more aggressive by nature than any other Caribbean nation so Lara was feeling very uneasy about that match. While we were warming up, we could hear plenty of anti-Lara banter coming from the stands. But Courtney very shrewdly diffused the situation by putting his arm around Brian when we took the field to bowl. That sent a message to the Jamaicans that Courtney did not have any hard feelings towards Brian Lara so they had no reason to either. Everyone simmered down after that. There were no issues in the dressing room, though a few of us felt Brian was too anxious to take the captaincy, but other than that there wasn't a problem. Courtney was not the type to go round talking up his chances or his leadership skills; he knew what leadership was all about after leading Jamaica and Gloucestershire and was no rookie as a captain. He had already led the team well in India as a stand-in, minus Richardson, Ambrose and Haynes, so he had earned his time in the job. All my five (official) West Indies captains were good in their own way. Viv was the most aggressive of the lot and wasn't afraid to let you have it if you weren't delivering. Whereas some captains might ask you what was wrong if you were not quite bowling like you should be, Viv would say, after checking if you were fit, 'What are you doing, man?!' more aggressively, but that was purely out of passion. Even though he was aggressive, Viv would still back you to get the job done; Richie was laid-back and quiet and would come to you to talk and would rarely raise his voice; Courtney was similar to Richie in that he was a good man-manager and would speak to you in a quiet, considered way; Brian was the most adventurous captain and, for me, was too adventurous. He would try weird things and set some strange fields but it was all out of his will to take wickets and try things. Brian would come to me and say, 'Ambi, let's try this plan or that plan' and quite often I would say, 'No, no, skipper, that doesn't sound right to me.' He understood the game very well but was overadventurous with his crazy field settings; Jimmy Adams was even quieter than Richie, though, given that he was surrounded by senior players like myself, Courtney and Brian Lara, I suspect he found it hard to assert his authority. He would *ask* us our opinion on plans quite often rather than *tell* us what the game plan was. It was good that he trusted us with our opinions but it sometimes demonstrated insecurity.

To be fair to Jimmy, though, none of my West Indies captains ever dictated what they wanted. It was more about passion and encouragement. Courtney was able to claim a 1-0 win in his first official series as skipper, after a ten-wicket win and then a draw. We expected to beat New Zealand, though they had a decent team with Nathan Astle, a good batsman, and Danny Morrison, who was a slippery customer with a fair bit of pace. We didn't expect them to give us much of a fight and that is how it played out.

By late 1996, the World Cup heartache was well and truly

gone from our minds, if not from our memories! We did, though, have the opportunity of some revenge with a tour of Australia. They had taken our Test crown in the Caribbean eighteen months earlier and had then hijacked our place in the World Cup final, even if we did self-destruct. We were falling behind the Australians but still felt we had a good enough team to go and beat them on their home soil, under the captaincy of Courtney Walsh. Guys like Jimmy Adams and Shivnarine Chanderpaul were now more experienced, while Brian Lara was a household name and certainly highly regarded in these parts after his masterly 277 four years earlier in Sydney.

The way this Frank Worrell series began perhaps typified the changing of the guard between both nations. Where we had once seemingly been able to recover from the most difficult of situations and still win, the boot was now on the other foot and they were showing those same never-say-die qualities that many in world cricket had not long ago regarded as West Indies' traits. In the first Test in Brisbane, we had them on the back foot at 196 for five but a fighting 161 by their wicketkeeper, Ian Healy, took the match away from us and changed the game completely. That didn't dampen our spirits and we felt we had enough in our ranks to pull it back like we had in 1992–93. We were unhappy to go 1-0 down that early but were still confident.

We took a hammer blow on a flat Sydney pitch to go 2-0 down after Warne and McGrath shared fourteen wickets. Warney did not need much assistance from the pitch but when there was some help he could be devastating. I have always admired Shane Warne over the years. I saw a few good leg-spinners in my career, including Pakistan's Abdul Qadir in my first series. Warne was the best, though, and not just because of the wickets he took. He could spin a ball so much. There was another Australian leggie, Stuart MacGill, who could also spin the ball quite appreciably but he never had the same control as Warne, who was a fantastic all-round cricketer who could bat and also catch well at slip. He was a complete cricketer and a fierce competitor, which was unusual for a spinner. It's not like he could bowl bouncers to back up his aggression like a fast bowler could, but he would give you a stare and say a few words; but then most of the Aussies liked to talk a lot. He was always coming at you and I admired him a great deal. I had the opportunity to play *with* him for an English exhibition side, Lashings, and we went to South Africa for a couple of games. I found Warney to be a good bloke who enjoys a laugh in the dressing room – like me – and I really appreciated my time with him. We spoke about the old days and by the time we played these games I had been retired for some time and I still managed to bowl a few quickish deliveries so Warney said to the guys, 'Imagine what we had to put up with a few years ago!'

Warne's partner in crime was Glenn McGrath and these guys were incredibly influential in Australia knocking us off our perch. Of course they had a wonderful batting line-up but much of the reason why Australia dominated world cricket was because of that Warne–McGrath partnership: two fantastic bowlers who could win you matches on any given day in any conditions. No matter how strong their batting might have been, they still had to bowl teams out twice to win games and series and these two were the guys most significant in Australia's success. They really made a difference. A lot of people have compared Glenn McGrath to myself over the years and it's a fair match-up. I would not argue with it as we're both very similar. Maybe I had a bit more pace and bounce in my earlier years but the way we bowled was based on the same philosophy. We could put the ball in the same spot all day, effortlessly, rather than spray it all over the place; our control was our greatest asset. And we managed to pick up wickets with that line of attack. I would suggest that I was a bit more aggressive with the ball and my stare and all that, while Glenn had more to say verbally, which is part of the Australian culture. I never had a problem with verbal aggression if it was designed to put a batsman off his game. Where I have a problem with sledging is when it becomes personal. I don't like that. And I'm not a fan of the excessive talking either. You can't be doing that every delivery. Whether it is personal or not I've always believed that too much sledging does not make any sense. Bowlers should let the ball do the talking for them. There's nothing wrong with the odd comment like if you go past the batsman's edge and you wish to inquire, 'Are you seeing this ball or not?' Simple quips like that are fine, but keep it short. If a bowler is good enough he should let the ball do the talking. A little confrontation is fine – spectators love it – but if it is too much it is not good for cricket.

We found ourselves under tremendous pressure at 2-0 down and knew it was going to be a tough ask to win the remaining three matches to win the series and reclaim the Frank Worrell Trophy. But we never gave up hope, which was one of our strong points. No matter how far behind in the contest we were, we always backed ourselves to come back. I must admit in the first two games I was not quite at my best. The Australians played well and I give them credit for that. But I was not firing, even though I was not conceding all that many runs. I was well aware of my lack of rhythm so prior to the third Test in Melbourne I put in some extra work in the nets. I was never afraid to spend hours in the nets, unlike the modern day guys who seem to favour the gym. A net session was my gym, my workout. That extra time on my game made all the difference and before we went into the Test I said to the guys, 'Gentlemen, don't worry, I'm taking ten in this match.' And I knew if I took ten we would win this game. I was feeling so confident. My body felt good and my bowling was where I wanted it to be again. When I was in that mood I felt invincible; unstoppable.

I believe that preparation is the key to success. The more prepared you are, the better your chances of getting those positive results that you're looking for. I have a saying that I use every time I'm coaching: 'Cricket is not like a light switch where you flick a switch on and it comes on. And you flick it off and the light goes out. Cricket is not like that.' You can't fool around, not train and expect to achieve good results. Every net session has to have a purpose. Work at your weaknesses to make them stronger. This is the way I approached that net session at the MCG and it helped me to go into the Test feeling good about my bowling: when your confidence is up you have more chance of taking wickets. I went out there and took five in the first innings (five for 55) and four in the second innings (four for 17). We won the game by six wickets but I was

disappointed because I did not live up to my word. I fell short
by one. On the upside, we won the match as we had to, to
keep ourselves in the series.

With my rhythm back and my best form rediscovered I was
on a real high, so was then incredibly frustrated to sustain an
injury in the tri-series final against Pakistan at the MCG, which
forced me to miss the fourth Test in Adelaide – a game we lost
by an innings and with it the series. It was hugely disappointing
to have to miss that game but there was no way I could have
played. I was hit on the inner thigh by a Waqar Younis delivery
in the ODI final. It was quite a new ball as I went in at 42 for
seven. The ball hit me that hard it left an indentation in my leg,
almost like a small hole. I received some treatment and batted
on and might even have won the match if Roland Holder had
stayed with me instead of getting run out. I finished 31 not out.
I came off the field, relaxed a little, cooled off and that's when
this injury worsened. For the next few days I couldn't walk!

I did everything I could to play in that fourth Test because I
knew how crucial it was: it was must-win if we were to take or
even draw the series. On the morning of the game I was still
trying to prove my fitness. I said to Courtney and the boys,
'Even if I can only amble in and bowl, I have to play this game.'
I felt that half fit I could still create some problems for the
Australians as much because of my reputation as anything.
Unfortunately, I went out there on the field and the pain was
too much. It didn't matter what our physio, Dennis Waight,
did, my body was just not responding. It was much more than
a bruise and was actually a serious leg injury. I could not even
walk properly let alone run. It was a huge blow to me and the

team given the importance of the match. I knew I was back to my best and would have been a handful. After my nine wickets in Melbourne, the Australians would have been lifted by my absence in Adelaide. I hoped the guys could at least draw the game so we could go to Perth, our lucky ground, and still be in the series. But it wasn't to be.

Typically, we did win in Perth, quite easily by ten wickets, but we lost the series 3-2. Courtney showed his greatness in Perth when he bowled off a short run-up while suffering with a hamstring injury and still took five for 74 at half pace. That was what I had hoped to do in the fourth Test but wasn't even able to do that much. In Perth, during Australia's second innings, I experienced something of a freak occurrence when I bowled nine no-balls in a fifteen-ball over. It wasn't a record I much wanted and to this day I am still trying to figure out what went wrong. I have not yet come up with an answer. I had taken five for 43 in the first innings so all seemed well with my game, but suddenly while bowling from the River End – into the wind – I kept overstepping the line. I tried to use my experience to put it right, like coming off a shorter run-up, but nothing worked. I slowed down my approach but still went over the line. I came around the wicket, still the same. Darrell Hair's right arm must have been aching with the number of times he had to signal no-ball. Halfway through the over I stood, placed an arm on Courtney's shoulder and asked him, 'Cuddy, man, what do I do next?' I suggested to Courtney that I bowl some off-spin just to finish the over but he said, rightly of course, 'Nah, Big Fella, that's not going to look good.' I couldn't understand it. After I finally managed to complete the over you can imagine the ironic cheers the Aussie crowd gave me. It wasn't very pleasant being the butt of everyone's laughter but I had to see the funny side and could do nothing but take off my cap and acknowledge the whole ground. I told Courtney I wanted to bowl another over just to prove, to myself more than anyone else, that there wasn't a problem. But he wasn't keen in case I had another over of torture. It hadn't happened before and didn't happen again. I do reflect occasionally how many of those were genuine no-balls. Was Darrell Hair just giving me a hard time? I'm sure he was right but for me at the time it was a disaster and hugely frustrating. I have heard it said that I bowled some of those no-balls on purpose and that I was trying to intimidate Andy Bichel with some short, hostile balls delivered from around the wicket, but that is nonsense. I would have done anything to stay within that front white line!

It was a respectable series result, losing 3-2, but did not ease the pain of another loss to the Australians.

Lara vs Tendulkar

'Lara took more chances when he was batting and was a bit of a showman, a crowd pleaser . . . Tendulkar will entertain you as well and play some great shots that will make you sit up and watch, but in a less flamboyant manner because he did not like to take chances'

It seems bizarre that although I made my Test debut in 1988 and Sachin Tendulkar made his a year later we did not actually face one another in a Test match until 1997. Anyone who knows me will tell you that I am not one who tries to make my life easier by avoiding bowling to the greatest batsmen around. I relished the contest against the best because I had supreme confidence in my ability as a fast bowler to give any batsman trouble. I didn't go hiding when Ricky Ponting or Steve Waugh were stroking the ball to all parts, or when Javed Miandad was gritting his way to a century. I always wanted to test my ability and character against the best players in the most challenging conditions and was pleased when Sachin and myself finally went to battle in the Caribbean when India toured. I am focusing on Sachin because of his incredible achievements over his career but that is no way meant as any disrespect to his team-mates like Rahul Dravid, V.V.S. Laxman and Sourav Ganguly, who were also fine batsmen. Tendulkar was just a cut above because of his supreme will to bat and bat. I had observed him from afar over the years and witnessed his development from a teenage prodigy, almost a schoolboy, into a great cricketer. Not only would he have been aware of the challenge against myself and Courtney Walsh in this series, but he also had to live with the comparisons between him and the other true batting great of the era, Brian Lara. This was something they both had to get used to through their parallel careers. The pre-series hype was all about Lara vs Tendulkar.

They were two different kinds of player; two greats who I would have in my side all the time. I would never want to compare them in terms of who was the better player because they were so different. Brian Lara took more chances when he was batting and was a bit of a showman. I don't mean that in a derogatory sense, I am simply referring to how he was a crowd pleaser, an entertainer. He would play more shots and be more adventurous in his stroke play. Tendulkar will entertain you as well and play some great shots that will make you sit up and watch, but in a less flamboyant manner because he did not like to take chances. They were both destroyers but in different ways. Their personalities are also very different. I know Brian better than I know Tendulkar but what I have observed is that Tendulkar has achieved a lot over the years and has always remained humble. That is a great quality to have as he could easily have become swell-headed through his status. He has never allowed his great career to go to his head or looked down on people, has always remained grounded, and I respect him for that. Brian is the opposite. He likes to have fun and party, have a drink or two. He is a very carefree kind of person and enjoys himself immensely. But I can tell you one thing: when Brian stepped over that rope he wanted to win 100 per cent and wanted to score big runs. Apart from moments on the 1995 England tour, which I have mentioned, Brian always gave everything for West Indies and caught well, fielded well and always got you runs.

Nets were always interesting when Lara and myself faced each other. We both had big reputations in the cricket world so naturally we're both very proud people and would not want the other to dominate. We were team-mates and were ultimately helping each other but our pride was also on the line. Lara never had a problem with nets, but if we started bowling too many short balls he would complain and say, 'Why all the short balls?' and that kind of thing. I would point out to him that when he got out into the middle and started receiving short balls, he couldn't ask them, 'Why?' It was his job to cope but he would protest that he shouldn't be facing so many short balls from his team-mates and asked for more pitched-up deliveries. I'd say, 'No, I'm not going to do that. When you're in the nets it's like being in the middle. If you can cope with these short balls on a regular basis, when you go out to the middle it will be a little easier for you.' It was the fast bowlers' way of keeping our batsmen honest and sharp. Not that Brian agreed. But it was the way I had operated right from the start in 1988 when me and Desi Haynes would almost play out a mini Test match in the nets.

Obviously I never knew what Tendulkar was like in the nets or the changing room as I did with Lara, but I know what he was like from 22 yards away. You hardly got a false stroke from him, which meant you knew you had to try and *get* him out because he wasn't going to give you his wicket from you just remaining patient with line and length balls. He would never try anything extravagant or out of the norm and give you a chance. If you bowl a couple of maidens to some players you can sense they're not happy to sit in and bide their time and will play a risky shot. Tendulkar's temperament was such that he was happy to wait until the right ball came along to hit. He would wear *you* down. You were not going to win against him from being patient because he had more patience than you. He could bat for a whole week, so you had to bowl *at* him. I always felt that I could get him out, even if it wasn't going to be easy. I would challenge myself, 'Get him out', because once you have dismissed him you know you have done something wonderful.

There are a few tricks we bowlers try to unsettle batsmen but you couldn't ruffle Tendulkar. I still gave him my stare as it was part of my game but I knew it was not going to work because he was such a composed person. You couldn't psych him out. He would go about his business like there was nothing else going on around him, apart from facing that ball. He had serious powers of concentration and I never saw him become emotional. If I saw him play a bad stroke, whereas some guys will hit their bat into the ground or their pads and chastise themselves, the most he would do was walk towards square leg to regain his composure.

This was my first Test series against India in eight years, due mainly to missing the tour over there in '94 through injury. The last time I played India was 1989 and Tendulkar was not then part of the team, with the mainstays being Ravi Shastri, Dilip Vengsarkar, Sanjay Manjrekar and Kapil Dev. By '97 it was time for the new brigade of Indian cricket, though Mohammad Azharuddin was still there. They were a good team, with a formidable batting line-up, but we believed we would beat them. If I'm honest I didn't have the best of tournaments and it wasn't the most exciting of series but when you are bowling to those guys your reputation is always on the line. I never wanted to have players come to my backyard and dominate me in front of the West Indian fans – not anywhere actually, but more so at home – so even if I wasn't taking many wickets, it was important that I kept a certain amount of control on the situation.

The first Test was a weather-affected draw. I didn't take any wickets in this match but at least my figures show what I referred to with regards to controlling the situation. I bowled twenty-five overs in the first innings for 35 runs. My attitude was if I'm not taking wickets, then I am not allowing any runs. I hated giving runs away. Franklyn Rose made his debut here on his home ground and bowled well, taking six in the first innings. Courtney and myself always tried to educate and inspire the new crop of fast bowlers because we knew we would not go on forever and West Indies needed good enough pace bowlers to succeed us. So we were pleased to see this early promise from Rose. I actually recommended him to Northants for the 1998 season. In time, Rose and a few others like Reon King, Nixon McLean and Mervyn Dillon disappointed me and Courtney with how they failed to grasp their chance of a long-term career in the West Indies team. They were all very good bowlers on their day but 'their day' never came round often enough and they all suffered with inconsistency.

Another draw followed in Trinidad, where we saw Navjot Sidhu compile an extremely painstaking 201 on what was a very slow pitch. I got him out bowled eventually but I had to work incredibly hard for my five for 87 (in forty-one overs). Tendulkar made his first serious contribution of the series with a patient 88. The duel between us was spoiled by the slow pitch as conditions favoured the batsmen too much but I still knew my reputation was at stake. I had bowled to him in one-day cricket before, like in the 1992 World Cup when I had to stamp my authority on him as the elder statesman. This was always going to be a totally different battle, one of attrition. I never did take Tendulkar's wicket here or in any of the five Tests we played together in our careers. It is unfortunate we only got to play this one series, purely through circumstances. I did take his edge a couple of times in Trinidad but the pitch was so slow the edges fell well short of the slip fielders. I got frustrated and started cursing. Not with him but with the pitch. 'What the hell is going on here?' When you take a good edge you expect the chance to carry through to the slips, but twice edges from Tendulkar's bat fell well short.

Tendulkar was in the runs again at Barbados with 92 in the third Test, which we won. This match was a thriller that we did well to come out on top in. They only needed 120 and we bowled them out for 81. Ian Bishop took four and me and Franklyn Rose three each. It was like a West Indies result of old, where we won with our backs well and truly against the wall. With their batting line-up we knew it was going to be a fight but our self-belief and will to win took us home. Other than this match it was quite a boring series, with the weather once again intervening to force draws in the final matches at Antigua and Guyana, where Tendulkar chalked up another 83. Their batting held firm for much of the series, apart from the one crucial innings when they should have won in Barbados. Dravid and Ganguly were different from Tendulkar because they would give you a chance and would occasionally play at deliveries they should not have played at. Tendulkar's lapses were few.

Atherton's England Humbled

'When they got hit on the glove, they started to act like they were in
Hollywood. I have always respected Alec Stewart as a good batsman but
I thought he was making a meal of it, shaking his glove and all kinds.
There was nothing dangerous in the pitch'

I decided to retire from cricket after we returned from the tour of Pakistan at the end of 1997. A 3-0 hammering over there was demoralising but that had nothing to do with my decision. It was more about my enjoyment not being there any more. The Pakistan tour certainly didn't help matters. We knew it would be a hard tour and a tough ask for us to beat them as many good teams had gone there and struggled. Even in 1990 with all our big names we could only draw the series. This time we had a solid team with Ambrose, Walsh and Bishop and a middle order of Lara, Hooper and Chanderpaul. But we knew Pakistan were difficult opponents. We always looked to win any series; however, on this occasion the coach, Malcolm Marshall, said if we couldn't win here then let us at least draw the series. But we never got going. They had some serious firepower in their bowling. The leg-spinner Mushtaq Ahmed bowled us out in the first Test with ten wickets and we lost by an innings. Things did not become any easier in the second Test in Rawalpindi when they unleashed their new pace sensation, Shoaib Akhtar – who came on first change after Wasim Akram and Waqar Younis. We thought things would get easier once those greats were out of the attack, but we were wrong.

It was the first time that we had seen Shoaib and he had blistering pace and completed a really potent attack. We didn't know who he was or what he was about, not like Wasim and Waqar. So he had a bit of mystery about him having seemingly come from nowhere and being even quicker than the two greats. We were like 'What?' He was fresh on the market and good for cricket. There is nothing more exciting than a real genuine quick who can bowl ninety miles per hour consistently to a great batsman: Shoaib to Lara; Thomson or Lillee to Viv Richards; that is what Test cricket should be all about. Any spectator would like to see such a contest. That attack was backed up by a good batting line-up with guys like Inzamam, Saeed Anwar and Aamir Sohail so they had a strong team. We lost the second Test by an innings once more and by the time of the third Test I was feeling a strain in my back. The series was gone so it was felt that there was no need to risk me and I missed the final match, which we lost by ten wickets. People complain about touring Pakistan but I found it OK, though I am a bit of a hotel junkie anyway and don't explore too much. The country was nice and the people were hospitable; it was just a shame about the cricket!

My plan on returning to the Caribbean was to play one last domestic season in the New Year for the Leeward Islands, try to win the first-class competition and finish on a high, and then officially retire from cricket. That would have meant not playing against England in the upcoming series, which was to be Brian Lara's first as the newly appointed captain, after he succeeded Courtney Walsh. Brian had heard the rumours about my retirement and flew out to see me in Barbados where I was playing for the Leeward Islands. Even though the news was already out, I had to deny the story publicly because I didn't like the way it was unfortunately leaked before I had the chance to speak to the WICB. I did admit to Brian when we sat down together, though, that the story was true and that I would be retiring because I was no longer keen to play cricket. He urged me to continue and said as a new captain he would need all the help he could get from the bowling department. Brian was very persuasive in convincing me that I was still a huge asset to the team and that he needed me to spearhead the attack, along with Courtney. I told him I would think about what he said. When I did eventually decide to play on it was not because of what Brian had said, although I appreciated his support and backing. It had more to do with me not wanting to go out with the retirement announcement being handled so clumsily and also, more significantly, because of my intention to prove a point to a few critics who felt I was all washed up.

Former Leeward Islands manager and Curtly's long-time mentor Hugh Gore said: 'I used to tell him that trials and tribulations make you stronger, and he always wanted to prove people wrong. The commentator Andrew Mason gave him a hard time when he went to Pakistan. He came back and answered his critics in the most positive way and started to bowl two yards faster. Self-motivation was a huge part of the player he was.'

That is not to say the belief invested in me from the skipper didn't mean anything. Of course it is always nice to have strong support from the captain as it gives you confidence. Brian and I got along very well and there were never any problems between us. I have already explained my feelings about his antics at certain times, as on the 1995 England tour, and his over-anxiousness to gain control of the team as captain. But generally we shared a good, honest relationship as team-mates. If I ever had to tell him something I would tell him – whether calmly or aggressively. We never had any issues as we played together for a long time and he knew me as a fair but also serious person who would speak his mind, against him or anyone else, if I saw something I didn't like. Brian appreciated how I was open and upfront. I was the same when he became captain because I know about fast bowling; I was not a rookie by then and figured my opinions should carry some weight.

So having opted to play on, there was the five-Test series against Mike Atherton's England to prepare for, which was to be my sixth Test series against England. This one began in Jamaica in the most calamitous of circumstances with an abandonment due to an unfit pitch. The history books show us that only sixty-two balls and fifty-six minutes were possible. For me it was a stupid decision to call the game off so early. They never gave the pitch a chance. It was a newly relaid pitch and if the umpires and match referee had doubts about it they should have called the groundsman to apply the heavy roller and try to put things right, or whatever else needed doing. They should have at least given the ground staff a chance to rectify their surface. If then after an hour of remedial work the pitch was still unfit, I would have accepted the decision to abandon the match. They called this game off after just an hour of talking. Thousands of England supporters had flown out to Jamaica and I felt they deserved better than an abandoned match without more effort to get this game on. It was a nonsense decision.

I was very disappointed with the West Indies Cricket Board for allowing the ICC to abandon this Test match, seemingly unopposed. I felt both organisations blundered. The way I look at it, you have Curtly Ambrose six foot eight, Courtney Walsh six foot six, a brand new ball at the start of a Test: it doesn't matter what surface you are playing on you are always going to get some bounce. That's a fact. Yes, there was some uneven bounce but it wasn't a dangerous pitch where it had to be abandoned. OK, the physio came on a few times but for blows on the gloves, not on the batsmen's heads. It is normal for me and Courtney to give batters a hard time at the start of a Test and hit them on the gloves. One or two kept low and a few jumped at the batsmen's gloves. But nothing flew up into the batmen's face. The bounce was nothing out of the ordinary. I have played in many games where there was uneven bounce and this game was no different.

If we were batting and were three down for 17 like England were, we would have continued and would not have complained about the pitch. We might say it's a terrible pitch but we would keep on playing. I take offence when people bang on about pitches in the Caribbean being low and slow and uneven and this and that. I don't like to hear people talk of West Indies being the only place in the world that prepares these pitches. I have played on worse pitches in England and other parts of the world. This Sabina Park surface was not as bad as Edgbaston in '95, which looked like a terrible pitch and played like a terrible pitch. And I've played at Perth when there were not what you would call cracks but actual potholes. In fact I was run out at the WACA in the 1996–97 series when I tried to run my bat in but it got stuck in one of the holes and I was unable to get over the line. I advanced down the wicket to Shane Warne, didn't get to the pitch, so I kicked it away and Ian Healy ran from behind the stumps to try to run me out. I should have got in easily but because of these holes I was run out. So these types of pitches are not uncommon. I felt really let down by the West Indies Cricket Board for not trying harder to keep this Test match going.

England skipper Mike Atherton countered: 'Edgbaston was a spicy pitch but nothing more. It was certainly a tough pitch to play good fast bowlers on. Jamaica, though, was simply unplayable. It was Brian Lara who called me on to the field and said he thought the pitch was too dangerous and we should call the game off. There was no way you could have played a whole Test on that pitch. I went back the next day and the cracks had lifted and disintegrated so there was nothing left of the pitch. There was little you could do to improve it. We got another Test added in Trinidad so common sense prevailed.'

The pitch was certainly not as bad as England made out. I wonder if England would have complained had they been 40 without loss, even though the physio might have come out a few times. Look at the three wickets to fall: Mike Atherton – played tentatively at a short and wide delivery from Courtney while trying to take his bat away and was caught in the gully by Sherwin Campbell: nothing wrong with the pitch there. Mark Butcher – to be fair to him he received a nasty delivery for his first ball that pitched short of a length but Butcher took his eye off the ball and a chance ballooned up to Stuart Williams in the slips: can't blame the pitch for that, only good bowling. Then I had Nasser Hussain caught at second slip from a typical Curtly Ambrose delivery just outside off stump: no blame should be attributed to the pitch there either. England made that pitch look worse than it actually was.

The reason this match was abandoned was because England came to the Caribbean thinking they had the best chance of beating the West Indies in years. Then they won the toss, decided to bat first and suddenly found themselves three down for nothing – Courtney had two, I had one. All of a sudden they thought 'this isn't working' and put on this big act. When they got hit on the glove, they started to act like they were in Hollywood. I have always respected Alec Stewart as a good batsman but I thought he was making a meal of it, shaking his glove and all kinds. There was nothing dangerous in the pitch. I know Alec Stewart and he was a tough cricketer; he would have battled on through this difficulty. Same with Atherton and Thorpe; I played against those guys for years and they were tough. I accept there were deliveries that misbehaved like one length ball from me that cleared the wicketkeeper's head, and one ball from the same area kept low soon after. I shared a smile or two with Stewart about it; we knew it wasn't a good surface. I am not saying this was a good pitch. I would just have liked to have seen more physical efforts made to do everything possible to keep this Test on.

Stewart recalled of that Test in which he was nine not out from twenty-six balls: 'The game should never have started. Somebody could have been seriously hurt and they knew that. Curtly bowled balls to me that we laughed about at the time – thankfully they didn't hit me. It was the worst track that I ever played on by a mile. It was far worse than Edgbaston in '95 and I opened the batting in both. At least they bounced at Edgbaston, but at Jamaica one ball would fly over the wicketkeeper's head from a length ball and the next from almost the same spot would shoot along the deck. I was doing my best to survive and Curtly knew it was an unfair contest. [Match referee] Barry Jarman took a bold decision but the right one.'

We left the field and sat there waiting in the dressing room for news of what was happening. All we knew was that there were discussions going on between the ICC and WICB about what to do. Then we got the news that the Test match had been abandoned – to my surprise. When we came off most of our guys expected some remedial work to go on with the pitch so we just relaxed and waited; an abandonment was the last thing on my mind. The WICB blundered badly. Barry Jarman might have called it off ultimately, but plenty of deliberations had gone on before that big decision was reached. The West Indies officials should have done everything in their power to keep this match on. We looked stupid to the rest of the cricket world and it was especially embarrassing for the local Jamaican Cricket Association.

The only positive to come out of that Jamaica game was that the ICC ruled the match would count in players' records and therefore the Hussain wicket was, apparently, my 309th so every cloud . . .! There was an extra game scheduled in Trinidad to compensate for the abandoned match. We won the first, and England the second. It was a bit of a competition between myself and Gus Fraser, who didn't bowl with much pace but was very accurate, very steady and always put the ball in the right slot. He took eleven and then nine in both matches and I managed eight in both. We went 2-1 up in Guyana, where I knocked over Mike Atherton twice in the game for nought and one to add to the pressure on him, which eventually told when he resigned after the final Test. I am not taking any credit for the resignation, though his own form and the team's eventual 3-1 loss in the series would no doubt have weighed heavily on his mind as he was a stubborn and proud man. If he was batting well and leading from the front, maybe he would have carried on. I dismissed him more than any other player in my career but I always respected him as a good player and regarded his wicket as an important one.

We drew in Barbados and won again at the ARG in what became the sixth Test, counting the abandoned match. The Antigua Test was heading for a draw but the fact we were able to win it by an innings demonstrates England's mood at that time. Nasser Hussain and Graham Thorpe were together after tea on the final day and were taking England to safety, but their big partnership (of 168) ended when Hussain was run out. I told Lara at tea the match seemed to be heading for a draw and that I didn't need to bowl any more, so I went out in my rubbers and didn't even bother to put my bowling boots on. Lara said, 'No problem.' But as soon as Hussain departed we quickly realised we still had a chance to win the game. I didn't get any more wickets but Courtney took another four to finish them off.

I was man of the series with thirty wickets and my prize was a car, a Rover 75, which I gave to Bridget, my fiancée, as we had planned to buy her a car at the end of the series. I took great satisfaction watching her drive that car around Antigua considering I was supposed to have been all washed up a couple of months before the series. It was a handy reminder to my critics that Curtly Ambrose was far from finished.

The South Africa Debacle

'It was a disastrous tour that started badly and was doomed to failure'

I was reinvigorated about my cricket following the 3-1 win over England in the Caribbean, having contemplated retirement beforehand. I even had the rare luxury of an extended period of relaxation afterwards now that I was no longer playing county cricket. But what I did not realise then was that I needed every minute of that rest as I was about to embark on the lowest and most stressful time of my career. The 1995 England tour was bad enough with a fair bit of infighting, but this 1998–99 tour to South Africa was simply painful on and off the field – from start to finish. It should have been a special, momentous occasion as it was West Indies' first Test tour there after the darker aspects of history, namely apartheid, meant this series was never possible – until now. The tour ended up making history of an altogether different kind as we lost 5-0 in the Test series and 6-1 in the one-day series that followed. Such dreadful results, though, were inevitable given that our preparation directly leading up to the tour had very little to do with playing good cricket in South Africa but served as a huge distraction. Quite simply, this tour was doomed to disaster.

It did not start on the right note, which is something of an understatement. West Indies played in the ICC Knockout (now called the ICC Champions Trophy) in Bangladesh, which directly preceded the South Africa trip that began in November, but Courtney and myself didn't go. We were supposed to fly to England from the Caribbean before meeting up with the rest of the guys in South Africa for the tour.

Prior to this series the team had some ongoing issues with the West Indies Cricket Board, which was then being led by Pat Rousseau (president) and Clarvis Joseph (vice-president). They were the ones we were appealing to. We felt we weren't being treated in a respectable way as professionals. What we were asking for was nothing unreasonable. The money that we were being paid at that time was lunch money, really. There were no annual retainers in those days, just tour fees. And we were not just looking out for ourselves either as one of the issues we had was the payments for the regional competitions. We felt it had to be more. It was a pittance really, but the scale of pay increased depending on how many Test matches you had played, with the guys who had never played for the West Indies at the bottom of the tree. For a four-day game for the Leeward Islands I'd earn something like US$400 – and I was in the top bracket. So imagine what those guys who had never played for West Indies were on. For a domestic one-day game I earned something like US$110. We started to tell them, 'You have got to do better than this', and we were well within our rights to say this as we were paid extremely poorly. Secondly, we were also trying to improve certain conditions. They had only just started flying us business class, as Wes Hall insisted, when he officially became WICB president, that we big fast bowlers couldn't be flying economy all the way to Australia and places like that. So it was taking our board a long time to catch up with the modern trends of how to treat your players. Things are better now thanks to the WIPA (West Indies Players' Association) but back then we felt we had to make a stand on certain issues.

We had been complaining about these things for a long time and it wasn't as though we suddenly started moaning. We just reached a point where we felt we needed to make our feelings known a little more vociferously. The board kept saying they would make things better but nothing would ever improve. We decided things would be different on this tour, after coming together weeks earlier during the Red Stripe Bowl, a domestic one-day series in Jamaica. A few of the senior players like myself, Courtney, Lara, Hooper and Jimmy got together and started to discuss the fees and we thought, 'Boy, we have been talking about this for quite a while now. Maybe it's time we took our complaints to the next level.' We were reluctant to swallow the board's empty promises any more and knew we had to take a stand to show them that we were serious about this. It didn't help matters that the board officials always flew first class, even around the Caribbean where there are limited first class seats. The message was that they looked after themselves but they didn't care about us. The guys then went off to Dhaka while Courtney and myself stayed back. I should say that although we were determined to raise the stakes, there were no plans for a strike at that point. Courtney and myself arrived in England and stayed at a London Heathrow hotel, the Excelsior, before our scheduled flight out to South Africa to join the guys. But before we did that we got a call from Lara and Hooper, who were still in Dhaka. They were the captain and vice-captain and were the ones taking a leading role in our protest, or mutiny if you believe some of the comments then. They decided that stronger action was needed.

This call was the first time that me and Courtney knew anything about what was to come. They informed us that they were not flying on to South Africa but were actually coming to see us in London to talk through these issues. Half of the squad actually landed at Heathrow instead of Johannesburg, leaving the other half to fly on to South Africa with the manager, Clive Lloyd. There was still no talk of a strike but I did get a sense that this was about to escalate as Lara and Hooper meant business after more fruitless talks with the board, who now realised something serious was afoot.

While Lara and Hooper were London-bound, the WICB had been tipped off, presumably by Clive Lloyd, about what was unravelling and they countered with a few tactics of their own. WICB member Joel Garner called me to say I should make sure I got on the plane to South Africa. He was clearly aware of what was cooking. I told him straight that if my captain and vice-captain were staying in London, how could I fly out without them? He said, 'Ma'an, who do you work for . . . Brian Lara?' I explained it was not a case of who I worked for but was about staying loyal to my leader and his second in line, who was Carl Hooper. Joel rang off by insisting I should be on the plane, but I didn't take much notice. My position was 'I work for the cricket board, yes, but I am for the team'. When Courtney, Lara, Hooper and myself sat down together to discuss our strategy, we soon realised that if we were going to make a statement it had to be as a whole team otherwise it didn't mean anything. I think it was Lara who then got word to the other guys in South Africa that they should catch a plane to London. Whether that was always Lara and Hooper's plan I am not sure but they obviously realised this stand would not work without the support of myself and Courtney as we were two senior players so they came to see us. All the guys came back – minus one player, Mervyn Dillon. Apparently he told the fellas that he couldn't find his passport so he couldn't travel. We didn't buy that. So that left the coach, Malcolm Marshall, and manager Clive Lloyd, along with Dillon. The word from the guys was that Marshall had got into Dillon's ear about staying over there with words like, 'Think about your career' and all that stuff, as they had always got along. In Dillon's position it would have been difficult for him to have ignored the advice of a man like Malcolm Marshall.

I was surprised there was no support from Marshall and the manager, Lloyd. They had been part of this squad not all that long ago and were aware of the issues we wanted to raise attention to. Lloyd came back to London when the stand-off intensified, though Marshall and Dillon never did return to the UK to be with the team, which was at odds with the WICB at the Excelsior for five days. My feeling was that even if you don't necessarily agree with the protest you have to back your team-mates and stay together, and I include Marshall and Lloyd in that. The fact they kept their distance and wanted no part in our strike created a 'them and us' atmosphere. Although Marshall was a huge influence on me when I came into the West Indies team, and though Lloyd was the godfather of West Indies cricket, guys in the team started to look at them a bit differently after this and not for the better.

Even with this stand-off over several days, nothing was ever resolved. I can't recall anything being written down or documented as regards better pay or conditions. It had gone on so long – it was just a huge feeding frenzy for the British and international media – we knew we had to finish this thing and had a decision to make: were we going to go on with the tour or scrap it altogether? I wasn't happy about the whole thing and was one of the first to speak out, against going on the tour. The board stood to lose a lot of money but that wasn't our main concern. Lara, Courtney, Hooper and a few of the younger guys like Stuart Williams agreed with me. We had been promised things for years by the board and nothing ever materialised so I figured that if still nothing had been agreed after this action then it was time to go home. Despite the senior players deciding we should not go, we never dictated or bullied anyone: it was always going to be a team decision. There were enough of the others who were not so sure so we decided it should go to a vote. Who was for going and who was not? Everybody had their chance to have their say with a vote between fourteen of us, because Dillon wasn't there. The result could not have been closer as it was an even split at 7-7. The seven for not going were Lara and Hooper, myself, Courtney, Stuart Williams, Franklyn Rose and Dinanath Ramnarine I said straight away, 'Guys, it's split 7-7, I'm not going. I'd prefer to head back to Antigua.' Seven of us were dead against the tour. But we were deadlocked and, despite my initial feelings, the more we discussed things I began to think, 'Boy, should we just go and do the tour?' I started to see things from the side of the other seven guys and we always did things in the best interests of the team so we eventually figured you cannot make such a radical decision as to scrap the tour if seven of our team-mates want to go: 10-4 in favour of not going would have made it easy to not go, but that wasn't the case. We started to come round to doing the tour just for the sake of West Indies cricket with the intention of settling our issues afterwards with the WICB as, by this stage, nothing had yet been agreed in writing with the board. So there it was; we reluctantly decided we were going to go.

Towards the back end of our stand-off, when things became real heated and as the WICB threatened to sack Lara and Hooper and even send a newly selected team, the South African cricket chief Ali Bacher flew out to see us in London to persuade us to go. He told us how Nelson Mandela was looking forward to seeing us in South Africa and played those political games to try and sway us. Of course we all respected President Mandela a huge amount; we all knew he was a great man. A few of us had met him already on our '93 tour to South Africa, when we played a tri-series. But none of this stand-off was ever meant to show a lack of respect to Nelson Mandela. Bacher was at least supportive of a full-strength West Indies making the tour. It was all a very messy situation, nonetheless.

There was not much time between that decisive meeting on a wintry Monday evening in London and the scheduled flight out to Johannesburg, so it was all a bit of a rush. Just when it seemed the situation could not get any worse, it did. By the time myself and Courtney came down into the hotel lobby, the bus had already left for the airport without us. Courtney said, 'Now what are we going to do?' I said, 'For me, this makes things worse. I didn't want to go anyway and had only agreed to go because of you guys talking me into it. And now two senior players – the leaders of the fast bowling pack – have been left behind at the team hotel!' I sat there in the lobby with my suitcase, seriously pissed off and wondering what to do next. I refuse to believe that Brian Lara or Carl Hooper would have chosen to leave us behind. We were the players who were going to bowl his team to victory. I blame the manager, Clive Lloyd. It is the manager's job to tell the bus driver when to leave and to find out if everyone is on the bus or not. Either the manager didn't realise we were not on the bus or he was pissed off with the whole thing and said, 'The guys aren't here, let's just go!' We decided to grab a taxi to meet the guys and by the time we reached the airport we had missed them and just about saw the tail end of the boys going through to security after check-in.

When we approached the counter a lady told us we were too late to board our flight and would have to fly the next day. It was getting worse and worse. We delayed our answer to the lady on the desk and said we would have a little think about what we were going to do. I sloped off and sat on my suitcase and talked to Courtney about our options. I was very tempted just to book a flight there and then and head back to Antigua. It could have been an innocent mistake to have left us at the hotel with all the hustle after the meeting, but then to have not waited for us at the airport either, not even the manager alone, it did not seem to be an accident. I felt as if Clive Lloyd was quite happy to leave us behind. He had to have taken a head count to make sure everyone was there. It was total and utter disrespect.

My mind was made up. My next stop was going to be Antigua. Courtney then pleaded with me to go and check back in at the hotel and fly out to South Africa the next morning, because the guys had already gone and he felt we couldn't abandon them – like we had been. Courtney is different from me; he can tolerate a lot more nonsense. It doesn't take me long to explode if something bothers me. Courtney is one of the few people in this world who can convince me to change my mind on something and eventually I backed down and agreed to return to the Excelsior and check in again before our flight the next day. Courtney and I were very bitter about what had happened and put the blame squarely on Clive Lloyd. Forget about the bus; we were peeved about that but it could have been an innocent oversight. There is no way, though, that he could have missed us at the airport as well. He blundered and we weren't happy about it. There wasn't even a message waiting for us at the hotel. It was as if we did not exist. I have no idea what Clive Lloyd's motivation was. We were not the ringleaders of this whole issue, which started in Dhaka when we were not even there. And Clive knew me pretty well; I was never any trouble for him or the team. This little episode was a complete mystery and still is.

We caught the flight the next day and finally arrived in South Africa. It is very strange that nothing was ever said about our late arrival and neither did we ask the manager what had gone on. We felt that after both of us missed the bus and then the flight it would be perfectly reasonable for the manager to inquire what the hell had gone wrong. It was pretty clear that myself and Courtney were not all that important to his agenda. We both grew up respecting and admiring Clive Lloyd – Courtney even played under his captaincy and, if I speak only for myself, I lost some respect for Lloyd over this. I was disappointed. It was all very weird.

If the preparation was bad, the cricket itself was a disaster. We played poorly on the tour and the tone was set from the final first-class match in Bloemfontein, before the first Test. Free State, after being bowled out for 67 in their first innings, needed 438 to win in the fourth innings – and got them! Hansie Cronje was 158 not out. It really said something about where our focus was at that time. Throughout that whole tour the problem lay with the batting department. The bowling was reasonable, sometimes very good, but most of the time the batting was very ordinary. Quite often Courtney and myself would take early wickets but the supporting bowlers were very inconsistent. They had a strong team, though, and Allan Donald and Shaun Pollock provided the backbone of their attack and caused us a lot of problems. I had played against them before in county cricket and knew they were good bowlers. Donald was pretty quick and while Pollock was not *as* quick, he swung the ball at decent pace. There were also the spinners Pat Symcox, Paul Adams and their great all-rounder, Jacques Kallis. This was my first good look at Kallis. At that time he wasn't the player he ended up being but you could see the potential. He was very Sachin-like as a batsman who gave you nothing and was a good bowler, too, and who could be sharp when he wanted to be. I always had a lot of respect for him, even at that stage in his career. I like to think I can identify special talent at a young age and I saw the greatness in Jacques Kallis then as I did in Sachin in 1990, and Brian Lara and Ricky Ponting in their rookie days also. My first impression of Kallis was simply that he was going to be a great player, purely from his potential. And now he has finished his career I can say with some certainty that Kallis is the best all-rounder I have ever seen. I never saw Sir Garfield Sobers play but everyone says he's the greatest so let's leave him out of this. From those I have seen, Kallis is better than Ian Botham, Kapil Dev, Imran Khan and Richard Hadlee, who are all true greats. Kallis stands above all of them, just ahead of Botham.

However strong South Africa were, we were simply not good enough, with bat or ball, but especially the bat. And we were never together collectively; there were too many divisions and I am not referring to the politics that went on back in England, I am talking purely cricket arguments. The bowlers were always complaining to the batsmen to do their jobs and it does cause division after a while. The second Test in Port Elizabeth is a good example. For a start, Philo Wallace pulled out before the game with illness and some of the guys were grumbling about his decision. I felt he was genuinely sick. But that illustrated the typical feeling of discontent around the group. In the match, we bowled South Africa out twice for 245 and 195, yet they bowled us out for 121 and 141. It wasn't good enough. I took eight for 79 in the match but we could never gain any advantage while the batsmen kept failing so badly. It didn't help either that we had two great cricketers – coach Malcolm Marshall and manager Clive Lloyd – who did not give us much support.

After we went 3-0 down in Durban, we held a very heated team meeting and I basically took over. I really lost it and couldn't take any more because our batting continued to struggle so much. I really ripped into the batsmen. My aggression had been building over time and now, with the series gone, this was the moment when I let the guys have it. I had some harsh words, especially, for Clayton Lambert and Philo Wallace, who looked like fish out of water. We played England earlier in 1998 when they had been aggressive, fearless and effective, so against South Africa I thought they would be the same players against the might of Allan Donald and Shaun Pollock; but not so. I told Lambert and Wallace how disappointed I was with them and said to their faces that they shouldn't play for West Indies again. I was really upset. I chastised them and also said that if at any time we are playing regional tournaments and either one of them tried to take me apart with their attacking game, I'm going to run halfway down the pitch and try to knock them out (with a bouncer). That's how they had always tried to play against me before.

Kent Libraries,
Registration and Archives
www.kent.gov.uk/libraries
Tel: 03000 41 31 31

Customer ID: *******4558

Items that you have borrowed

Title: Curtly Ambrose : time to talk
ID: C333926044
Due: 08 September 2022

Total items: 1
Account balance: £0.00
Borrowed: 1
Overdue: 0
Reservation requests: 0
Ready for collection: 0
18/08/2022 13.53

Thank you for using self service

But they seemed timid against Donald and Pollock and I told them in no uncertain terms that I didn't appreciate their sudden retreat into their shells. It was disrespectful to me, as though they feared Donald and Pollock more, and it was certainly disrespectful to the team, which was relying on them to come out all guns blazing and show some fight.

In that same meeting I also chastised Carl Hooper greatly. I saw Hoops in the nets on a few occasions on that South Africa tour with the bowling machine set to bowl short-pitched deliveries at him and he was heavily padded up. But over all the years I had played with him, which was a decade by then, I had never seen that before. He was never like that. It was clear that he was intimidated by South Africa's pace bowling and I ripped into him for being so timid. There was total silence while I was saying my piece, which is normal, because the guys know when I am in that kind of mood people sit and listen until I'm finished. I have hardly ever been interrupted. The guys know I don't chastise them for no reason. I turned to the captain, Brian Lara. I told him he was too good a player to get starts and not carry it on and instead give it away. Normally when Brian's set he's extremely hard to get out. I told him to take more responsibility. I hammered those four guys, though Brian to a lesser degree because he was at least chipping in with fifties if nothing else. I didn't touch on the younger guys too much. I felt they did the best they could in those circumstances. I also directed a few words, though not so harsh, towards some of the bowlers like Merv Dillon, Nixon McLean and Franklyn Rose. I told them they needed to step up as they were not backing me and Courtney up enough.

Nothing much changed after my outburst; if anything, the batting became worse. At Centurion in the fifth Test we were 102 for two in our first innings, courtesy of a stand of 97 between Brian Lara and Shivnarine Chanderpaul, yet were bowled out for 144! I didn't play in that final Test because I had a swollen left knee, which I sustained in Port Elizabeth. I strapped it and iced it before every session but wanted to keep on playing because we were still in the series. Even after the series was gone when we were 3-0 down I wanted to play through the pain to try and make it 3-2 to win back some pride. But at 4-0 down I figured I couldn't go through the pain barrier any more. And I also wanted to rest in order to regain my fitness for the seven-match one-day series that was coming up so that we could salvage something from the tour. Not that the one-day results were any different. I have lost series before but that South Africa tour was the lowest point of my career – from start to the finish. It was simply a disastrous tour that started badly and was doomed to failure. We should have gone home after the stand-off in London. It would have cost the WICB some money but there were just too many divisions in the team for us to be successful. Very few positives came from this nightmare of a tour.

Bouncing Back

'Whenever people talk of the great Australian batsmen I hear Bradman,
Border, the Chappell brothers, but rarely does Ponting's name come up
and that surprises me because he was a great player . . . for pure
batsmanship, Ponting was by far a better player than Steve Waugh'

We had a month between the morale-sapping tour of South Africa and the upcoming challenge of Australia in the Caribbean to rid ourselves of all the negativity and bad habits we had developed over those three months in South Africa. It was a tough ask. That tour had been a complete nightmare but we knew it was no good dwelling on it and we had to regain some confidence in our cricket and claw back some credibility with the West Indian fans. Once I got away from South Africa I was able to spend a short time at home and began to put that experience behind me – though you don't forget those kinds of defeats because they hurt – a lot. The natural competitor in me was determined to come back hard against Australia. It was a new challenge and something I needed to refocus on as much as the team did. It was going to be another tough series, of course, especially after they managed back-to-back wins over us in the last two series.

We approached the Test series with our captain Brian Lara's future in some doubt, which I think had as much to do with the stand-off with the board before the South Africa tour as much as the results from those Test and one-day series. He was given the captaincy for only the first two Tests of the four-match series against Australia, so he was basically on trial, which was a little bit strange to us. In my career up to then a captain was selected for the series, not for part of a series. This was just another example of the WICB's short-term planning that could have no positive impact on the team. It suggested there was no faith in Brian Lara as skipper so he was under unnecessary pressure, initially. That edginess from the board was reflected in our performance in the first Test in Trinidad. Glenn McGrath took ten wickets in the match and cleaned us up badly. The manner of our defeat did not look good as we collapsed to 51 all out in nineteen overs. They bowled well but not well enough to excuse that batting display. We should have batted much better. There were similarities between this game and what had gone on in South Africa with the batting failures, as we managed to bowl the Australians out for reasonable totals here in Trinidad, for 269 and 261.

It was the worst possible start, and not what we needed after South Africa and with our captain under severe pressure to keep his job. I had some sympathy for Courtney, who took his 400th Test wicket but in bitter-sweet circumstances. It was now six Test defeats on the bounce and if we ever needed some inspiration from our captain, this was it. Thankfully, he didn't let us down. We showed good character to bounce back in Jamaica with a ten-wicket win. Brian cracked a magnificent 213 and put on over 300 with Jimmy Adams (94). They were two brilliant innings and proved we had character and were not going to lie down and play dead. This was after it looked like we were sliding to more embarrassment when we lost four early wickets. That partnership gave a lot of confidence to the team. We badly needed it and it was a turning point in the series.

We moved on to Barbados feeling extremely confident while the captain was also given the job for the last two Tests of the series, but that was always likely after his brilliant innings at Sabina, which really set the tone for our newfound belief. The fact that Australia won the toss, made 490 and still lost this game shows how far we had come in such a short space of time. It is amazing what a win can do for a team's confidence. The Test in Barbados was one of the most dramatic games of my career as we snatched it by one wicket. Early on, though, it seemed as if we might dominate a bit more when they were 36 for three. But that man Steve Waugh (199) came together with Ricky Ponting (104) and changed the game around. They really made us toil and must have enjoyed it more after we did the same to them in Jamaica with that big partnership between Lara and Adams. I had already identified Ponting's talent before this series and I knew he would be great. When a lot of youngsters came up against the West Indies teams I played in they were often timid and looked to just find their feet. He wasn't one of those guys but took the attack to us. So I recognised his confidence and ability. I've always admired

Ponting highly and felt he's been underrated over the years. Whenever people talk of the great Australian batsmen I hear Bradman, Border, the Chappell brothers, but rarely does Ponting's name come up and that surprises me because he was a great player. As good a competitor as Steve Waugh was, no disrespect intended, for pure batsmanship Ponting was by far the better player. Both had big hearts and huge character and would not back down. But their character was displayed in different ways. Ponting would always take you on. Steve Waugh would not give in either, instead looking to battle it out and look for survival rather than going after you. Once he sticks around and wears you down, then he scores his runs.

This game culminated in a run chase where we required 308 to win. Again the stage was set for Brian Lara to showcase his greatness and he didn't let us down. He was dropped a couple of times but this was undoubtedly one of his best innings when you consider the magnitude of the series, the strength of the opposition and the way they went after him. Brian held the innings together brilliantly but, if I may say so, my contribution with the bat was also quite important. I came in at number ten when we were 248 for eight and still needing another sixty for victory. I only scored twelve but I held my end up while Brian dragged us closer to the finishing line. Thankfully there were no 'Caddick moments' this time, unlike in '94, and I batted for almost an hour and a half. My job was simply not to get out. With only Courtney to come we couldn't take any chances. West Indies' last hope lay with me and Brian, who told me that he was going to give me one ball every over and he was going to face five and look to score. I told him, 'No, skipper, you don't need to shield me. If you can get one run off the first delivery, take it. I can handle this thing.' But he stuck to his preferred plan. He did explain that it wasn't because he thought I couldn't do it but he wanted to take responsibility himself to get the job done. Right through our partnership he achieved that aim. Every fifth delivery he got a single, even if the field was in close. It was genius how he found a gap every time. There were occasions when we thought about a third run but settled on two so he remained on strike. Our plan worked brilliantly. The Aussies were frustrated and tried desperately to get me out. There weren't too many short balls because they would have been a waste. I would just have swayed out of the way. So they were bowling wicket to wicket and trying to get me out bowled, lbw or caught behind or in the slip cordon. They never said anything to me throughout this partnership but then again they never did say anything to me normally. Why would you? Dean Jones tried it once and look what happened!

One of the few times Lara didn't get his single I had to face Jason Gillespie from the start of the next over. By now we had put on fifty-four and were just six runs away from victory. Before that over began Brian was really annoyed with himself that he hadn't managed the single to take the strike. I reassured him and said I was OK. But I wasn't. The third ball of the over from Gillespie was short and wide of off stump and I couldn't make up my mind whether to leave it or to slap it over point. I was caught in two minds and eventually just hung my bat out tentatively and guided it to Matthew Elliott at fourth slip. It was a nothing shot and I was disgusted with myself. The ball was ripe for a slash over point but because of the tense situation and the need to keep my wicket I became hesitant and it cost me. I took my time walking off the field and met Courtney on the way off. I told him he had three deliveries to survive and that he shouldn't try anything extravagant because Brian would get the runs at the other end. I sat on the steps of the pavilion (as you could at the old Kensington Oval, not like it is today) with my pads still on and watched each ball to the end. Every ball Courtney blocked was met with a big cheer and he survived the over. Lara took care of business after that, with a four through extra cover to win the game. It was pandemonium in the dressing room; a magnificent Test match and won by one of the finest innings you will see by Brian Lara. He had an ongoing battle with McGrath and they were saying things to each other and I think they even brushed against one another at one point. It was Test cricket at its best with great players going to battle for their country. Thankfully we won this one, if not the war. It was a nice feeling to lead the series 2-1 but reclaiming our number one status was not in our thoughts as we had fallen too far behind Australia by now. Winning the Frank Worrell Trophy and a series win was very much on our minds, though.

We felt we had one hand on the trophy when we reached Antigua, but sadly we were unable to see out the job and lost. I managed eight wickets in this match but not scoring enough first innings runs cost us. The ARG was flat for the majority of my career so we should not have been bowled out for just over 200 in both innings. We didn't play well and should have at least looked to draw the match to hold on to what would have been an unbelievable series win. Brian scored another hundred to cap what was a magnificent series for him. He didn't get enough support from his fellow batsmen throughout and the fact we ended 2-2 spoke volumes for just how significant his runs were. I was doubly disappointed not to win back the Frank Worrell Trophy because I knew this would be my last series against the Australians and I wanted to go out against them on a winning note. Retirement had been floating around in my head, seriously, since the start of 1998 so by now I knew I would not be making another tour of Australia. On a positive note, I was proud with how we fought back from going 1-0 down after the 51 all out in Trinidad to then lead the series 2-1. That showed a lot of character and I took much satisfaction out of that. We were up against a great team and to finish level after four Tests was some achievement. Overall, from my six series against Australia I am able to boast that I finished 3-2 up, so I still have some bragging rights over Warney, McGrath, the Waugh brothers and the like!

The ensuing one-day series ended 3-3 plus a tie, while some unruly crowd behaviour was witnessed in Guyana and Barbados. I was rested for part of the series, missing three games, but came back for the seventh match in Barbados in place of Carl Hooper, who retired suddenly from cricket after the match the day before. It was all very strange. It seems like the whole of Barbados loves Carl Hooper. I think that love for him stems from the time he went there as a young man to play for Guyana against strong Barbados line-ups in the early 1990s and scored hundreds at Kensington in successive years, against Malcolm Marshall, Ezra Moseley and Franklyn Stephenson. We're talking serious pace and quality in that line-up and he watched the fear in the dressing room before going into bat, but went in, played a few shots and won the admiration of the Barbados crowd from there on. He could do no wrong for the Bajans – some even branded him Sir Carl. But when he played in the sixth one-day international against Australia at Barbados in '99, he had put on a bit of weight and was rather sluggish in the outfield. He was fielding at short midwicket and normally in that position the old Carl Hooper would have swooped on the ball, but this time he didn't make much of an effort for some that came his way and was signalling to the man on the midwicket boundary that it was his ball. It happened quite a few times during the game and the Barbados public lost it with him and started heckling him real badly about his weight and said he was lazy. He couldn't take it from the crowd he thought adored him.

At the end of the game the boys came off the field and, to our shock and amazement, Carl announced to us in the dressing room that he was going to retire from cricket. Just like that. I understand he later denied he quit because of the heckling but I feel he was acting on his emotions straight after the game, which I thought was immature. Maybe he was also falling out of love with the game, I don't know, but I couldn't understand it and was disappointed as we lost a quality player. I thought it was a cheap way to retire and it also dropped us in it just before the 1999 World Cup. He could have made a difference with his batting and bowling, and experience, especially of English conditions after three Test tours there plus all his county seasons at Kent. It is interesting, though, how things can turn around in West Indies cricket for he came back again in 2001 – as captain.

So we went into the 1999 World Cup without Hooper. This was my third and final World Cup and it didn't go well. We never made it through the preliminary round. We began with a defeat to Pakistan when we had another look at Shoaib Akhtar, who bowled extremely quick. I remember him bowling a bouncer to Sherwin Campbell – a very good hooker – and it hit his bat before he had time to react and went over third man for six. His figures may not be flattering but he bowled at a very lively pace, on a juicy pitch as well. I missed our next match against Bangladesh in Dublin because I felt a little niggle in the warm-up, but it was a match we felt we should win anyway. It was a good one to miss because it was freezing cold. I sat in the dressing room with several jumpers on trying to avoid the wicked breeze that was blowing through the ground. We went on to beat New Zealand and Scotland but a loss to Australia meant we were going home. Apart from my freakish figures of two for eight in ten overs against the Scottish, there's very little to talk about from this forgettable tournament, which was a shame actually after our impressive 2-2 Test series and 3-3 one-day series draws against Australia. I missed the tour of New Zealand later in the year, after injuring my arm in a one-day series in Sharjah. So by the time 2000 came round, with my new custom-built home, I knew the end was near.

Farewell

'Headingley was a disaster of a game,
probably the worst I've ever played in'

I knew 2000 would be my final year in cricket although my intended exit was delayed until the end of the England tour. It felt the right time, as I explained earlier, even though I knew I was still good enough to go on. I always wanted to go out on my terms and while I was still bowling well. Hopefully my statistics support this after I played in all seven of Leeward Islands' first-class matches, taking 31 wickets (at an average of 12), including four for 18 from sixteen overs against Jamaica in the final that was drawn. Not bad for an old man!

When I wasn't playing cricket I was attending to the final touches of my house that I had built in Antigua. I was still living with my mother at this time and moved in with Bridget in 2001 when we were married. Because I was on the road for nine or ten months a year I did not feel it was worth living together before then as I was hardly ever home. By 1999 I had started to build my house at Cedar Valley and it was all completed at the start of 2000. I was given an acre of land by the Antiguan government of the day, the Antigua Labour Party (ALP), as a gift for my contribution to cricket and for promoting Antigua & Barbuda at the highest level. I chose that piece of land after the Land Office gave me several options around the island. It's a nice, quiet area on the edge of the Cedar Valley golf course. Richie Richardson lives near, further up into the Valley. It's not uncommon to have a few golfers walking by shouting 'Ambi, what's up?' when I am on my porch.

It probably sounds weird that I live right next to a golf course and yet I have barely played the game. I have actually tried golf and been on the range but have never taken it too seriously. I was in the minority amongst the West Indies guys as someone who never really bothered with golf. Desmond Haynes, Jeffrey Dujon, Viv, Brian Lara, Richie Richardson, Sir Garfield Sobers, of course, and many others – they're all very good golfers. In fact, Courtney Walsh was in Antigua one day and wanted to play some golf. I am an honorary member at Cedar Valley Golf Club so he wanted me to arrange it. As I'm not much of a golfer I called my friend Ian Edwards (who's a low handicapper) to have a round with Cuddy. I took a cart and followed them around and watched them play. In doing so, I looked at Cuddy and thought, 'If Courtney can play golf, then I can play golf, too', because I am a better athlete and more coordinated than him. So shortly after that time, while on a family vacation in New Jersey, I set about becoming more serious about golf. I asked Desmond Haynes to write down for me all the clubs that I would need because I didn't have a clue.

In New Jersey I bought myself some extended, left-handed clubs with the glove, bag and all the gear. Desi, who has a very good sense of humour, also listed various clothing items that I would need and he wrote on the bottom of this piece of paper, 'If you find you're no good, at least you will look the part!' I got back to Antigua with my new clubs and took to the range with Ian and started hitting them well. Viv, who spends so much time on the course like Richie, was there and stood watching me, 'Hey, Big Fella, looking good, you need to get on the course,' he said. I still haven't really dedicated much time to the golf but I have my clubs and will do one day. The guys keep telling me once I get started I will be hooked. I have a DVD to help me understand the technical aspects a bit better. Eventually I will enjoy the golf but my leisure time has been limited with various commitments like my music and coaching and so on. I don't want to start for one week and then not be able to play for three months, I want a long run at it and it will happen!

I enjoy fishing, which is one of my favourite pastimes, but, more than anything I enjoy spending leisure time with friends. I will occasionally meet up with Ballu at his workplace and just to prove to him that I'm not out of touch and can still change a few tyres! In fact, it was while I was at the garage when an architect dropped by and showed his plans off to the guys. I saw this drawing of a house he had designed and was impressed. We got talking and eventually he designed my house as well. The guy who built it was an old friend from Swetes so it all came together quickly and was under construction while I was overseas in Sharjah towards the back end of '99. Before Bridget, myself and the girls moved in, I had my pastor drop by to say a blessing for the house. I do the same every time I buy a new vehicle, before I start driving it around. It's just a matter of giving thanks to the Almighty for blessing me with my cricket talents. I always give thanks. These things were embedded in me from my mother while growing up and I never changed. My children are now the same and go to church and choir practice, always taking part in church activities. That's how we are.

West Indies' first series of the year was against an underrated Zimbabwe in March. I approached the series and the one that followed against Pakistan knowing they would be my last. And I had made up my mind that I wasn't going to England. I say Zimbabwe were underrated with good reason. They had a decent team with Heath Streak, Andy Flower and Murray Goodwin. In the first Test in Trinidad we could have lost as they had us on the ropes. We went into that series with the mentality that they couldn't beat us – but they very nearly did. They were chasing only 99 to win yet we bowled them out for 63. I was glad to play my part with three for eight in eleven overs but I have to say Franklyn Rose changed the game (with four for 19), with the wickets of Goodwin and Andy Flower. It was a very disciplined bowling performance like in the old days; we were determined not to lose this match. Once they got so close to us we knew we had to stamp our authority on them in the second Test in Jamaica. No disrespect meant, but we had it in our minds that Zimbabwe couldn't come to our backyard and give us a shiver; that couldn't work. We needed to show that we might be down on our fortunes but we were still ahead of them. I bowled tight in Jamaica but one strange quirk of my career is that I never took more than two wickets in an innings at Sabina Park in my eight Tests there. It's weird because Jamaica is like a second home to me and I have always felt comfortable there. I've been well looked after all around the Caribbean but since my international debut in Jamaica in 1988 it felt like another home. It's more special now that Courtney and myself are like brothers, so we hang out whenever I'm there. I wasn't sorry to see the back of my one-day international career after taking one wicket from my last six in the tri-series against Zimbabwe and the other touring team Pakistan, to whom we lost in the final.

The main event, the Test series against a strong Pakistan that boasted the likes of Wasim Akram, Waqar Younis, Mushtaq Ahmed, Saqlain Mushtaq, Inzamam and Yousuf, began with a bore draw at Guyana. The same result followed at Barbados, though it was refreshing to see Wavell Hinds announce himself against such a potent Pakistani attack with 165. We had suffered so badly through batting collapses in these times that whenever a youngster threatened to emerge it was exciting. This was also the Test debut of Ramnaresh Sarwan, who scored 84 and went on to have a good Test career, if not fulfilling his early promise. Wavell's fellow Jamaican Chris Gayle was introduced that year also yet I felt Wavell was the better player. We all know how things turned out, with Gayle blossoming into a world-class player, so it's no good continuing that debate, but that's how highly I rated Wavell back then.

After those two draws, it was do or die at the ARG. This was the time when I told Courtney we would be together for the last time. He worked on me throughout the match to change my mind (as explained in the first chapter). The great Wasim Akram used his box of tricks to take eleven wickets on a pretty flat deck – he swung the ball round corners. It was a real nail-biter of a Test and Jimmy Adams and Courtney took us to victory by one wicket, with Courtney sticking around for over an hour at the crease. Who would have known he could bat for so long? He took us to a 1-0 win – and without Brian Lara, who was having issues with the WICB. That was going to be it for me. That was me and cricket done at 388 Test wickets. But as I've detailed, Cuddy talked me into going to England. I really do have him to thank for reaching 405.

> Mike Atherton, Curtly's long-time adversary, had this to say about his bowling
> nine years after he first confronted him in a Test: 'He wasn't as quick by 2000
> but was still as accurate and still as miserly, probably more so. What he couldn't
> do by this stage was turn on that explosive spell that he could earlier in his
> career, like the seven for one at Perth. He lacked that extra dimension he once
> had, but that's a natural evolution for every fast bowler.'

Lara sorted out his differences with the board and was restored to the squad that toured England, which was obviously a huge boost. Whatever his off-field issues might have been, and there were a few over the years, any team would always want a batsman like Brian Lara in their ranks. It was fitting, too, that my old team-mates were there on the coaching staff, with Roger Harper staying on as coach and Jeffrey Dujon as his assistant. The nucleus of the team still looked strong with myself and Courtney leading the bowling, and Lara, Chanderpaul and skipper Jimmy Adams forming what should have been a solid middle order. The series began perfectly with a win inside two and a half days at Edgbaston. But our batsmen – again – somehow messed up at Lord's in the next Test when we should have taken a 2-0 lead. It was a disaster, the first of two such cases in this series. We had a 130-run first-innings lead and were well in the ascendancy until we were skittled for 54 all out in our second innings. The England bowlers performed well, especially Darren Gough, Dominic Cork and Andrew Caddick, but we shot ourselves in the foot. Sherwin Campbell was caught at third man while cutting so we didn't do ourselves any favours. And by this stage Campbell had been in the team for six years and could no longer be called a rookie. The rot set in then. We kept losing wickets and never recovered. I was angry, real angry, but there was no fighting or arguments in the dressing room. We stuck together, went out there and fought hard and very nearly won, with England only narrowly getting home (at 191 for eight). We really gave it a go. Courtney took ten in the match and I took five and didn't give anything away either. Those fifteen wickets that Courtney and myself shared out of eighteen proved yet again how the supporting bowlers, Reon King and Franklyn Rose, didn't step up, which was a familiar theme of the series.

I returned home between the second and third Tests while they played the one-day series, as I hadn't seen the family much with the home series directly preceding the England tour. When I returned to England I had with me Bridget and the girls, Tanya and Chloe, as I thought, this is my last tour and it would be nice to take my family. So they remained with me for the rest of the tour. We struggled again with inconsistency in the batting and bowling departments in the third Test, which was drawn. Our bowling was all about myself and Courtney, with Rose and King not stepping up enough. The opportunity was there for these guys to grab a West Indies career for themselves – Courtney and myself could not have supported them more. But you cannot bowl *for* them. They had the pace and the ability but were just not consistent and it was very frustrating for us both and the team. England's bowling, though, was firing as a unit, with Gough, Caddick, Cork and also Craig White. A typical Brian Lara hundred led the way in the second innings as we fought to compete. Sadly, with the series poised at 1-1, we failed to take the initiative and our worst moment still lay ahead of us.

Curtly took a call midway through this England series from his loyal friend Winston Benjamin, at a time when the West Indies Cricket Board were still hopeful of persuading him to stay on beyond the England tour. 'I said, "Listen, Ambi, I saw something today that didn't use to happen. You bowled short to [Michael] Vaughan and he pulled you. You tried to retaliate and it wasn't working. Forget the extra year they're talking about – time to call it a day." I had played with him a long time and didn't want him to undo all the great standards he had set for himself.'

The fourth Test at Headingley was a disaster of a game, probably the worst I've ever played in. It was bitter-sweet because I took my 400th Test wicket there. I said to the guys when I was on 399 that I wanted it to be either Atherton or Stewart because of our battles over the years. I wasn't bothered about Graham Thorpe or Nasser Hussain or anyone else. No disrespect to them, I would have been happy with any wicket but I felt it would be nice if it could be one of my long-time adversaries like Atherton or Stewart because of the respect I had for them. Atherton was favourite because he was in first and indeed it was him, caught Lara at first slip. That was fitting in my opinion.

England were 105 for five at the end of the first day, after we made 172, and my evening was a quiet one with Bridget and the girls. The recognition from the crowd for my achievement felt nice – from both the West Indian and English supporters – and I didn't feel like I needed to be celebrating too hard that night in the middle of a Test. That wasn't my style anyway. A quiet family dinner at our Leeds hotel was enough for me. I would never have guessed, while on the way to the ground for day two, that the game would finish that day. Caddick completely destroyed us with four wickets in one over. Darren Gough, who was a good, slippery bowler and could bowl sharp, did the damage upfront by ripping out the top order. Gough had a big heart and would run in for his captain all day. Caddick didn't ease up either and finished off the job with an inspired spell of bowling, removing the rest of us in the middle and lower order. Our batting was terribly inconsistent again – bowled out for 54 at Lord's and now 61 at Headingley.

Nobody was lambasted in the dressing room but we did talk about the poor way in which the guys were batting. We knew they were better than that. Sometimes those conversations were heated but we were all in it together and knew we had to stay as a group to improve things. Myself and Courtney were very aware that we were no longer sharing a dressing room with Desmond Haynes, Gordon Greenidge, Viv Richards and Richie Richardson. In those days you could be brutally honest if a guy had messed up because we all knew he was better than that. But by 2000 Courtney and myself were more likely to be hard on ourselves than the youngsters. We wanted to lead from the front and carry the young players. We took on a lot of responsibility, though at Headingley it was the batsmen who had messed up. It was the likes of Brian Lara and Jimmy Adams who had to lead from the front. But it is no good being too hard on guys who are still learning their trade like Adrian Griffith, Sherwin Campbell to a lesser extent, Wavell Hinds and Ramnaresh Sarwan, who was actually not out in both innings at Leeds anyway. You can be aggressive and passionate without turning on individuals. I would tell all of them, 'Come on, this is the West Indies cricket team, you have to pay more attention to your game and work a bit harder' – that kind of thing. You can hammer them but still do it in a constructive way, to remind them of the honour associated with representing West Indies, which maybe is forgotten a little too easily sometimes. I would say my piece and once we leave the dressing room it is all forgotten and we are one again. This series just summed up the continuing transition of our team, which was about to become a whole lot harder when I bowed out after the fifth Test, to be followed by Courtney a year after. We badly missed the grit of Shivnarine Chanderpaul at Leeds and the flair and experience of Carl Hooper, who was still in international exile.

A miserable series was completed at The Oval with yet another England win for a 3-1 series triumph – their first over us in thirty-one years. Even there we might have been looking at worse humiliation when my wicket saw us stumble to 75 for eight in the first innings but we scrambled past 100. Apart from the flattering guard of honour that Nasser Hussain's team arranged for me when I came out to bat on that final Monday afternoon, it wasn't the way I would have chosen to end my cricket career. But it was a pretty good journey overall.

Sir Curtly: The Afterlife

'[On being told of my knighthood]
I didn't know what to say – I thought it was a prank'

I was in Barbados, coaching the Combined Campuses and Colleges team – a good initiative that introduced another side into our first-class competition – when I received a call from the Antiguan Governor General's office. A gentleman on the line advised me there was going to be a special occasion in St John's, Antigua, on 28 February (2014) and that I 'had' to be in Antigua then, no matter what. I was supposed to be going to St Kitts with the CCC team for a game starting 1 March, so my initial reaction was that I could not be there. I had no idea what he was referring to and asked him what it was all about. He said he would get back to me so I took it as nothing and wasn't actually planning on going. What was strange, though, was that Andy Roberts had phoned me beforehand asking if I had received a call from the Governor General's office. I said, 'No, I didn't get no call from them.' Andy rang off with the words, 'OK, expect a call.' I left it at that. I later found out Andy knew what it was all about but he didn't wish to tell me. This guy from the Governor General's office eventually came back to me and wanted to confirm that I was going to be in Antigua on the 28th. I asked him again to give me more information and he then volunteered the words, *'Ambi, it's only fair to tell you that you are going to be knighted'* and went on to say it would be at the halfway interval in the game between West Indies and England; me, Richie Richardson and Andy Roberts, together. His words stunned me. I didn't know what to say and my first reaction was that it was a prank. He repeated himself but I was still not buying it. But eventually he convinced me and I assured him I would be there because it was a huge honour.

They had not announced it officially by that stage so he asked me to keep it confidential for the time being and ended the call with words that I will never forget: 'We want to announce it officially first so don't even tell the woman you are sleeping next to at night.' So, naturally, I went home and told Bridget. She is my wife, after all, and deserved to hear it from me rather than through the media. Bridget almost found out before I did. She had bumped into Andy Roberts at the supermarket a few days before and he later told me he almost told her the news but realised that we didn't know anything about it so he refrained. It was very humbling, though I do feel myself, Andy Roberts and Richie Richardson have done more than enough to promote Antigua (& Barbuda) to deserve the honour, which was eventually bestowed on us at the Sir Vivian Richards Stadium by Governor General Dame Louise Lake-Tack. I was so busy with my coaching commitments that I barely had enough time to let my mother and family know about the knighthood. They were obviously all very proud and it's a nice thing to happen to the family when you consider our background and the struggle in the early days. I like to think it is proof that a lot of hard work and an equal amount of pride, mixed with talent, can take you a long way. I had received other prestigious awards but nothing like a knighthood. I received the Order of Antigua (OH) in 1992, and the Grand Cross of the Most Illustrious Order of Merit (GCM) in 2003. While in terms of my cricket, I was inducted into the International Cricket Council's Hall of Fame in 2011.

Many Antiguans, and especially those from Swetes Village, shared his pride when he became 'Sir Curtly Ambrose', as former team-mate Enoch Lewis commented: 'Antiguans love Curtly and were so proud of him when he was knighted but the people from Swetes were even more proud. Nobody from the village had ever made it to Test level before him so he had to carve out his own path. Yes, he took advice, but Curtly made his own way. He could easily have given up. That's where his influences helped him, like his friend Ballu, who recognised he had a talent and encouraged him; otherwise he might still be changing tyres.'

I had no regrets entering my retirement from cricket and it felt good at first to be able to do what I wanted, enjoy my newly built house, move my family in and just go about life as I wanted rather than have to follow a schedule handed to me by the West Indies Cricket Board. It was a huge honour for me to play for West Indies for twelve and a half years and I feel great pride in my achievements and those of the team. But we have to move on and I was ready for the next stage of my life. Music was to be a big part of that, as you will learn in the next chapter, but it was also a time for me to enjoy my family. I had been on the road for so long. I had received other prestigious awards but nothing like a knighthood. I received the Order of Antigua (OH) in 1992, and the Grand Cross of the Most Illustrious Order of Merit (GCM) in 2003. While in terms of my cricket, I was inducted into the International Cricket Council's Hall of Fame in 2011.

Bridget and I had met in 1988 yet were not married until 2001, once cricket was firmly eradicated from my day-to-day life. The ceremony, on 4 July, was led by Revd Cortroy Jarvis at the Spring Gardens Moravian Church in St John's – call it neutral territory if you like as my family's regular church is the Cana Moravian Church in Swetes – where we still go now on Sundays. Bridget wasn't a Moravian – she was an Anglican from All Saints Village, which is near to Swetes. The pastor was actually from Swetes and played cricket there as a fast bowler before my time, so it was very much a fast bowlers' celebration! My brother Danny came over from his home in New Jersey to be my best man, my unofficial brother Courtney Walsh came over from Jamaica, my long-time friends Winston and Kenny Benjamin were there, though Richie Richardson and Viv Richards couldn't make it. Most of my old friends were there, like Hugh Gore, Ian Edwards and Ballu, as well as all my close family. It was a good day.

Married life didn't change my routine much though music became an even bigger part of my life once these days of leisure kicked in. I expect golf will also become a part of life but not just yet. I can't say I missed cricket all that much and certainly didn't watch much on the television but I never was a big watcher of the game. I might take in half an hour here and there but I have never been one to sit in front of the TV all day and watch cricket. That's just not me. But as time passed, and as my years in retirement increased, I started to receive the occasional offer to give me a route back into cricket. I reluctantly tried commentary and actually enjoyed it, despite my initial reservations. I started with radio for the Test match between West Indies and Australia at the Sir Vivian Richards Stadium in 2008. I have since worked on television also. It's interesting to see the game from a different perspective and to have to analyse the whole match rather than just see it from your own point of view as a fast bowler.

Since taking a back seat, in the time I was out of the game so much changed in cricket at elite level, globally. Twenty20 has obviously become a huge growth area for our sport. I've heard people say from time to time that T20 'will take over' eventually and gradually become the dominant focus of international cricket. I don't share that view. Test cricket is and will always be the pinnacle for me. It is also the only format you can be fairly judged on at the end of your career. Your status can only come from how many runs you have scored or wickets you have taken in the Test arena. Nobody will ever become an all-time great from playing just T20 or even fifty-over cricket. Therefore, I hope the International Cricket Council continue to support the prestige of Test matches.

I do believe, though, that Twenty20, whether it is the Indian Premier League, Big Bash, Caribbean Premier League or whatever, has a part to play in the ongoing marketing of cricket.

It is exciting and the spectators love it. I see T20 as a stepping stone towards ODIs and Test cricket. When players have success in T20, spectators should be curious as to whether those players can transfer their abilities to the longer formats. And the challenge for players is to do just that. If they succeed then that is good for them, but if they struggle to adapt then they're branded as T20 or limited-overs specialists, which is what I feel they should be looking to avoid; but I suppose many players now don't mind playing just Twenty20 and earning the riches it brings. But this is not the way I would see it if I were them.

Test cricket is the genuine article to show just how good a cricketer you are; you will be found out pretty quickly against the top sides if your game is not equipped to survive at that level. But in T20 you can play extravagantly and be lucky more times than you would be in a Test match. Test cricket examines your technique and your character – do you have the temperament to go out and play a long innings in a tough situation? Can you take wickets on a good batting pitch when your team is up against it? Only Test cricket will ask these kinds of questions. Yes, T20 serves a good purpose in modern cricket: it's lucrative, it's entertaining, it brings new fans to the game and it does encourage players to develop new skills. I have enjoyed my time coaching in the Caribbean Premier League (CPL). I have no problem with T20 at all. But for me a Test match is the purest form of cricket and is the truest examination of who you are as a cricketer.

In terms of my coaching career, I was pleased to take on a role in 2012 with the Combined Campuses and Colleges team, which was based at the University of the West Indies (UWI) at

Cave Hill in Barbados. Sir Hilary Beckles, currently the vice-chancellor, was a driving force in recruiting me and it was nice to be wanted. I felt I had something to offer and most of these players were rookies; I figured they could benefit from my advice and guidance, so I jumped into that role. It only came about after I got a call from the former West Indies player Floyd Reifer. He was the player-coach of the team. Discussions between him and Sir Hilary centred around me being part of the team's infrastructure, as assistant coach. I wasn't doing much coaching at the time so I decided to go for it, after convincing myself that I would not mind being around long days at the cricket again! It was actually Bridget who urged me to do it because she felt that the Antigua and Leeward Islands teams had ignored me up to that point, for over twelve years, and this was my opportunity to prove myself as a coach. I had already gained a Level II WICB coaching certificate (my plan is to go through and be certified at all levels) so I had always left that door open to future opportunities. I went to see Hugh Gore before accepting the job, as I value his advice. My loyal friends from down the years, like Ballu, Ian and Maurice Francis, all said the same thing. I relied on advice from my closest friends because I was aware that I had been exploited down the years with no agent and I wanted to ensure I was doing the right thing.

Floyd Reifer was still playing when I took the job and he said from the outset, 'Ambi, you run the thing.' So between the two of us we planned all the sessions. For the second year we added Corey Collymore to the coaching team; he was a great addition. I enjoyed the challenge of coaching and trying to develop cricketers into becoming better. I was given respect by the players. Some of the guys are already coming through the system now, like Jason Holder. He was a wonderful young man to work with, very respectful and hugely talented. I believe he has the ability to be very good. He swings it and has good pace though we are working towards trying to help him bowl a little quicker. He has time on his side so hopefully we can be successful in that regard. The Jamaican wicketkeeper-batsman Chadwick Walton is another who passed through the CCC system to good effect, as have Carlos Brathwaite, Jonathan Carter and many more. The CCC team has been dropped from the West Indies Cricket Board's new vision for franchise-based domestic cricket, which is a shame and extremely disappointing. The team has proved itself competitive since it began in 2008 and has defeated all the traditional regional teams – some more than once – with the exception of Jamaica. Some of these players' territories watched their progress with CCC and then came calling so they could draft them into their own teams. The CCC initiative served a good purpose in the development of young players who could not gain entry into their territorial teams and also handed them a university education.

Through my experiences with the Combined Campuses and Colleges, I felt like I was now into the whole coaching thing, so it was not too hard a decision when Ottis Gibson asked me to join him on the coaching staff of the West Indies team, as the bowling consultant. My old friend from the Leeward Islands and West Indies teams, Stuart Williams, was the batting consultant, with Richie Richardson team manager. I joined up with the West Indies team in May 2014 on Ottis's recommendation. I was happy to get involved if people felt that my contribution could help to make West Indies cricket better. I had played, and even roomed, with Ottis, so I knew him and he knew me well and what I had to offer. It was a shame when he parted company with the team shortly after I started work, but we all know coaching is like that: your destiny is not always in your own hands. I worked on the home series against New Zealand and Bangladesh in 2014 and at the time of writing was in India, with a busy schedule ahead of me, including a tour of South Africa and then the 2015 World Cup.

I have no problems with the players and have worked with captain Denesh Ramdin in the CPL so we know each other. I met our one-day captain, Dwayne Bravo, many years ago when he first came on the scene playing for Trinidad as a youngster. He came up and introduced himself to me. We were on the same flight and we talked all the way from Jamaica to Antigua. He tried to pick my brains on cricket and bowling and all that stuff and I was impressed by his will to learn and develop his game. We really hit it off and have remained friendly ever since. Even now that he's a renowned international star he will still ask me what I think of his bowling or his cricket generally. He is humble and respectful and was very happy to have me as part of the team. Any decision about my contract lies with the WICB, but he was insistent that I stayed on as part of the coaching set-up, so it is good to be wanted by the guys. Over the years many of the players have gravitated towards me even though I've never worked with them before, so working with the players was an easy transition for me.

Curtly's mentor Hugh Gore was delighted to see his return to cricket, at a time when music was the focal point in his life. 'I saw him all through his career but I get equal pride when I see him now, mentoring the Guyana Amazon Warriors in the CPL and the West Indies team, like when he was with the Combined Campuses in Barbados. He is able to pass on his knowledge in a way people appreciate. When he was offered the West Indies bowling coach job, he asked me for my opinion. I told him he had to take it as it was a wonderful opportunity and that he should not be intimidated by the people with all the certificates. His qualification is experience – he motivates people.'

I am excited about the future, my own and that of the West Indies team, because we have enough talent in the Caribbean to climb back up the rankings. But I feel we need to talk about reaching the top three, not being so unrealistically ambitious as speaking of number one at this stage. You have to get to number three before you can be number one. We do seem to play better in the shorter formats, but I still think that we are good enough to win Test matches and series because most of these guys who play well in one-day cricket are good enough to adapt to Test matches as well. The talent is definitely there to be competitive enough to win Test series. I believe that and we are working towards that. It is unfair that reporters or cricket fans in general always ask, 'When will West Indies get back to where they were in the 1980s?' It is nonsense to think like that. From 1976 right up to 1995 we were the dominant team in world cricket and for fifteen of those years, from 1980 to 1995, we didn't even lose a series. How many teams in world cricket or even sport generally dominate consistently for a twenty-year period? It's unheard of. How can a team do those things?

We were a group of islands that bossed the cricket world, with very little in the way of infrastructure, through pride, talent and a will to win. It was an amazing run of success. And my argument is, how can anyone possibly compare teams from that generation to what we have now? Yes, mistakes were made over the years in failing to invest in our future development, but there is still talent there and there always will be. You can't expect that golden generation to come again. We are talking about the best team that cricket has ever seen. It is unfair to expect any modern-day West Indies team to emulate the success of what we had back in the 1980s. It's an impossible comparison. We are not going to see that type of cricket again. One or two players may yet come through and dominate world cricket and do as well as some of those guys did before. But from a team perspective, we are not going to see that again. It was a freakish period where so many greats came together in one generation. The same thing happened to Australia with Shane Warne, Glenn McGrath, Adam Gilchrist, Ricky Ponting, Steve Waugh and so on. You get these cycles occasionally and you cannot expect whatever team you have from the present day to emulate the achievements of those kinds of players.

What I do know is that we have enough talent in our playing resources to dominate world cricket. It won't happen for fifteen years but we can be on top again. Of course, it will take time as we are way down in the rankings. I am a realist and feel we should first target the top three as you can't be thinking about number one when you are seven or eight. At least when you're in second or third position you're just a place or two away from being top dog. That is what I'm trying to teach the guys. You can't be a world champion overnight. You have to work your arses off and climb steadily before the top position is in sight.

The controversial India tour that was cancelled after only three one-day internationals at the back end of 2014 was a sad blow to our attempted climb back up the world ladder. I say sad not only because of the potentially huge ramifications – financial and practical – but because I genuinely felt our squad was strong enough to win in India. We don't manage that too often nowadays, in fact not many teams do, as India has always been a difficult place to go to and win. Unfortunately injury kept me out of the 1994 tour to India, so this tour would have been my second chance to at least be involved and contribute towards a West Indies Test series in India, which is such a great country to tour because of the passion and appetite the spectators there have for the game.

I was not directly involved with the politics of the cancellation, or even the build-up to it, but I was privy to some team meetings in which the players and management discussed the situation. All I can say is the team management – myself, team manager Richie Richardson and interim coach Stuart Williams – all appealed to the players to put aside their differences with the WICB and the West Indies Players' Association and commit to the tour as scheduled. Make no mistake, we wanted the tour to go ahead so I was disappointed that there was no compromise reached between the players, the WICB and WIPA. The players gave us respect and listened to our views but the final decision was down to them. We sympathised with them. Look, we have been players and know what can happen where contracts are concerned. Nobody needs to remind me that I found myself in a similar scenario back in 1998 when we almost didn't go ahead with the South Africa tour. But we played that even though I didn't want to at the time. Ultimately the cricket has to come first and the differences can always be resolved later, but on this occasion cricket, especially West Indies cricket, was the victim and this was a travesty. Hopefully the Indian board will not hold a grudge against West Indies because we have always had a very special relationship and enjoyed our battles together down the years.

Back to our rankings and the team's plight from here, there are many reasons why West Indies cricket is in the lowly position it is in right now and one that does not get much of a mention is the lack of mentors, inside the dressing room. When you lose all your great players in a relatively short space of time there is nobody left to inspire or show the youngsters the way. Brian Lara was there for a while before his retirement. Shivnarine Chanderpaul is still there but there has been a lack of senior players. In the bowling department especially you once had young bowlers like Jerome Taylor, Tino Best and Fidel Edwards trying to learn the art of fast bowling on their own, without the guidance of any experience around them. It has been the same with the batting to a lesser degree. This is a significant factor in the decline. Back in the glory days not only was there talent around to replace talent but there were also mentors in the team to help nurture those rookies. Courtney Walsh had Garner, Marshall and Holding. I had Marshall, Walsh and Viv. Before us Marshall had Roberts, Holding and

Croft. Desmond Haynes replaced Roy Fredericks and had Gordon Greenidge. Richie Richardson replaced Larry Gomes and had Viv. It happened time and again. Brian Lara replaced Viv and had Richie and Desi around him. Even when Marshall retired, Courtney and I tried to nurture the likes of Franklyn Rose, Reon King and these guys. That has not been the case for many years now. There has been a generation of struggling youngsters with no one to teach them the ropes. So it is important that the likes of Chris Gayle can be role models for the next generation. He has a lot of experience that can be of huge benefit to the youngsters coming into the team.

We in the Caribbean, and maybe even cricket in general, have this nasty habit of saying once you're past thirty or thirty-two you are old. But that is nonsense. If the player is fit and looks after himself he can go on and resume a very important place as an older, experienced head in the team. If you have a team full of youngsters, who is going to teach them the way? A great team always has a good balance between youth and experience. When we speak of Chris Gayle we hear about how explosive he is in Twenty20 and, yes, of course he is. But he is also a quality batsman in the Test arena as his two triple centuries will testify. Too many people overlook his Test record because of the danger he poses and his success in T20. He can still offer West Indies a great deal as we look to develop the next generation.

One thing that does have to change, too, is the attitude from players and officials towards our domestic cricket. I wrote earlier of the intensity of the domestic cricket scene that I knew early on, especially when my Leeward Islands team played a star-studded Barbados in '88. I don't like to compare eras but it appears that the guys in the modern day are not playing with the same level of passion that we played with. I'm not saying they're not passionate about what they are doing or don't care, but sometimes it does look that way. That inter-island rivalry in days of old was one of the significant reasons why West Indies were so strong: it was do or die. If you weren't up for the fight as a batsman you would be pummelled. And as a bowler, if you weren't focused, you could be taken to pieces and humiliated. That competitive spirit domestically was replicated on the international stage.

That passion I and guys from my era played with is still remembered now and appreciated. I played a game for the West Indies Masters against England Masters years after my retirement at the Kensington Oval with Greenidge, Viv, Hooper, Walsh and the rest. What was interesting was just how well we were received by the crowd. It was clear that they still love us and perhaps is an indication of their frustrations concerning West Indies' struggles since that team faded away. Our fans have been denied the chance to see winning cricket in internationals on a consistent basis and they are knowledgeable people. In this match I refer to, they acknowledged our contribution when we appeared for what were merely exhibition matches. The cricket meant very little really but the esteem in which we were still held was heart-warming and meant a great deal. I distinctly remember Viv saying to me on the bus, while driving into the ground and seeing the hundreds of fans lining up to welcome us, 'Hey, Big Fella, it's like being back in the glory days.' It demonstrates the volatile nature of the West Indian cricket fan and the culture in the Caribbean. One day you feel they are against you for whatever political reason it might be on the day, but at another time you can feel their pride in what we have achieved on the cricket field as a group of nations that came together and united for the sake of cricket. Our great sport has caused and continues to create discord through the politics and insularity of local rivalries throughout the Caribbean. But, equally, nothing binds West Indians more closely together than cricket.

Music and Me

*'The very first song I learned was "Stir It Up" by Bob Marley.
I liked the bass line, it was nice and sweet'*

Music has been an active passion of mine for as long as I can remember. My preference is for calypso and reggae, with Culture and Peter Tosh my favourites, though I can enjoy any type of music, even rock. Bob Marley is the greatest of them all and is above any debate. Outside of Marley, Peter Tosh ranks highest. He was sadly killed at his home in 1987 but he left a huge legacy. His songs were often against the system, with strong anti-establishment lyrics, and I always admired him for standing by what he believed in. I never got to see Peter Tosh because of his untimely death but I have seen Culture a few times. Other favourite artists of mine include the South African singer Lucky Dube and Jamaican reggae artist Beres Hammond, who I now consider a close friend.

I came to know Beres through his fellow Jamaican and our mutual friend, Courtney Walsh. He was putting on a show at the After Dark nightclub in the Saint Lawrence Gap, Barbados, in the mid-nineties while the West Indies were playing a Test match at the same time. Most of the guys went to the show and in fact he called Cuddy and myself up on stage, which I didn't really like too much because I prefer to keep a low profile. He told the audience that he liked to watch us bowl and said we were the main reason he watched cricket, which was very kind of him, but a little uncomfortable for me. We met up with Beres at the team hotel, Club Rockley in the south, as Courtney enjoyed his music and he wanted me to meet him because he knew I was playing bass. We have remained friends since then and whenever I go to Jamaica, Cuddy and myself go to his house to talk about music and chill out. I've never jammed with him but I have been with him when he's working on songs, as he has a studio in his house. I enjoy the fact I have a circle of friends outside cricket. Steven 'Cat' Coore, the guitarist from another famous Jamaican band, Third World, is also a personal friend of mine and my new band, Spirited, did a gig in Antigua with them.

Music has always been a part of me from when I was a little boy growing up, listening to music and enjoying live bands. Long before cricket, at home in Swetes, I manufactured some makeshift drums from old milk tins that I would put on the end of a stick and beat, so my musical juices were flowing at an early age! Bass guitar soon became an instrument I focused on, though I appreciated the brass section like saxophones, horns and so on. We used to cut the heads off bottles of Clorox bleach and join two together with a piece of plastic and blow it like a trumpet or saxophone. Me and my younger brother

Jamie would play around with these makeshift instruments as youngsters and I would usually try to find the melodies out of the Clorox bottles. So you could say I gravitated towards music early in life.

That appreciation never really developed into anything practical for many years. It took rooming with my West Indies team-mate and fellow Antiguan Richie Richardson to change that. Richie and I used to room together before he became captain; the 1991 England tour was the first occasion. Richie had played guitar for quite a few years. On tour it was his way of relaxing while living in the high-pressured atmosphere of international cricket, just to get away from the game. I used to listen and wish that I could play music. Richie had played for quite a few years and he started to show me where the notes are. He would strum his guitar and I used to hit the table as if it was a drum kit and I would sing, too, because Richie never wanted to sing. We used to enjoy those mini jams. I really got into it and by the time we reached Birmingham I was ready to follow Richie into music and buy an instrument to call my own. There was a musical instrument shop around the corner from our hotel and, out of the blue, I said to Richie, 'You know what, I am going to buy a bass guitar.' When I used to watch live bands I would always focus on the bass player but I had never played a proper instrument in my life up to then. So me and Richie walked to this shop and I bought my first bass, a black headless Steinberger, which means (to the uninitiated) the tuning pegs were at the bottom of the guitar and not on the head like normal. Those kinds of basses were the in thing in those days. I bought that style of bass because of a band I was into, back in Antigua, called the Burning Flames. The bass player from that band, David Edwards, always used a headless bass and made it look so easy. He was my idol so obviously if I was going to buy a bass I was going to buy a headless like him. In fact, as soon as I became more proficient on my bass, the first calypso song I learned to play was 'Island Girl' by the Burning Flames.

When Richie became captain of the West Indies he was given a room on his own so we would practise there and he would always have a mini amp on him. Most evenings after a game we would play a few songs; it was a good way to chill out after a tough day's cricket. The first song I learned was 'Stir It Up' by Bob Marley. I liked the bass line, it was nice and sweet. While Richie was the first to show me the notes on my bass, my first proper music tutor was Everton Benjamin, brother of the West Indies fast bowler and my good friend Kenny Benjamin. As an aside, Kenny and his brothers were all named after famous West Indies cricketers. There's Kenneth Charlie Griffith, Everton (after Everton Weekes), and there is another called Rohan (after Rohan Kanhai). Everton was in another of my favourite bands in Antigua called the LA Crew. I knew him very well and once he heard I was playing bass he was keen to help me and wrote down all the notes for me to learn. I used to take that sheet of paper with me everywhere. I'd put the paper away and test myself and see what I could remember, because if you want to be a musician you must know where the notes are.

In those days, the early to mid-nineties, I would practise with Richie on tour and then return home and link up with

Everton. If there was a song I was desperate to play, he would teach me, whether it was calypso or reggae. After a while Richie and I started to make guest appearances on stage with the LA Crew because we had become friendly with all the guys. You could sense the surprise in the crowd once people started noticing that we could play our instruments. They were very impressed and started to pay some attention to us. It was like 'Man, Richie and Ambi have some talent.' Sometimes, I'd sing with the LA Crew, which was something I did naturally from the days of fooling around in Richie's hotel room on tour. I will never forget the time one of their singers, Glenroy 'Zamba' Richards, turned to me after and said, 'Ambi, you have got a lot of talent, to be able to play bass and sing at the same time. It's not easy.' I was a little embarrassed and told him not to try and make me feel good just because I am Curtly Ambrose. But he insisted he meant what he said and that gave me a lot of confidence. Quite a few other people have said the same thing to me over the years, though it was a skill that came natural to me. Not many play bass and sing at the same time. The likes of Sir Paul McCartney and Sting are two well-known examples. I am quite happy with that company: Sting, Sir Paul McCartney and . . . Curtly Ambrose. It certainly makes a change from being compared to fast bowlers!

The Burning Flames, for me, were the best group in Antigua and they became huge influences on me and Richie. They consisted of three brothers and a nephew. Clarence 'Oungku' Edwards was their keyboardist and vocalist, Toriano 'Onion' Edwards was the guitarist and vocalist, David 'Krocuss' Edwards was the bass man and their nephew Ronnie 'Fox'

Watkins was the drummer. We used to go jamming with these guys all the time and it made us feel really good because Richie would learn a few things from the guitarist and David Edwards would teach me some bass. It was like me and Richie were living a double life. Cricket was business for us, our day job that we loved and what paid the bills, but music gave us an extra buzz that is difficult to describe. Music has never been about money; it is about enjoyment. The Burning Flames were great musicians and I felt privileged to be jamming with them. Being international cricketers would certainly have helped us to meet them, but I still feel they would have given us their time if we were not household names. But being a famous cricketer helped no doubt. I said to David Edwards one day, 'I have my bass but I need a new one.' He replied, in his husky voice, 'No problem, Ambi, anything for you.' And he gave me another one, as simple as that. This one had a (tuning) head on it. If I wasn't who I am he might have been reluctant so I accept that my celebrity has helped me with certain things over the years. I cherished that bass.

Music was still fun for me and Richie but things took on a more serious edge after we guested for another band called the Dread and the Bald Head. I knew the lead singer very well. He was a Rastafarian by the name of Davison Benjamin but was more commonly known as 'Bankers' – his stage name, if you like. He used to give me their CDs and would sign them and we became quite friendly. He learned that Richie and I could play music so we did a few gigs with his band. The keyboardist, Gavin, had a shaven head – hence the 'Bald Head' in the band name. After Richie and I had been away with the West Indies, we learned the band had split. They were no more and Richie and I started joking that it was our fault. As soon as we started playing some music with them, they broke up. Bankers, though, called a meeting with us soon after and he told us that he wanted to reform the band – with Richie and myself. I immediately refused this flattering offer because I was still quite insecure about my musical ability as it had not been all that long ago since I was a rookie and these guys were serious recording artists.

My grand plan was to retire from cricket and go to music school in the US, and actually learn to read sheet music and become an accomplished musician. Only then would I think about joining a band. I was also concerned about the amount of rehearsing we would need to do because it is one thing going up on stage and playing a couple of songs but when you're in a band you have to perform for a couple of hours. It's hard work. I honestly did not think I was good enough to be in a band then. Bankers continued to reassure me that I would be fine with enough practice. This gave me a problem because when I'm confronted with a challenge – and this was a serious challenge – I rarely walk away from it. I have lived for challenges my whole life. So I decided to give up on my music school plan, for now, and take my chances and jump in with the band, which was now called the Big Bad Dread and the Bald Head. I thought I could learn as I went along and maybe even combine my commitments with the band with some random music classes.

We launched the band privately in December 2001 and immediately started to rehearse. By New Year's Day we were ready to let the world know because we had practised and played a few songs together, though I was uncomfortable and reluctant about doing that so quickly. We played our first gig at a bar Richie used to co-own called Lashings in the north-west side of Antigua. That was the official start of my music career! We became a famous band around Antigua and toured throughout the Caribbean to locations like Grenada and Barbados; we even went to New York, and also played the World Travel Market at the Excel Centre in London twice as myself, Richie and Viv would often go there to promote Antigua & Barbuda. We got Viv up on stage to sing once and that was great fun. So the band was going well. Of course me and Richie gave the band a certain amount of marketability and we would not have done many of these international gigs if we were not part of the group. Bankers knew this and welcomed the added profile.

But after seven years and making three albums together, in 2009, which was an election year, Bankers decided he'd had enough and wanted to change career and move into politics. I tried to talk him out of it but he had been a musician for so long and he fancied a change of scenery and a new challenge. From that moment the Big Bad Dread and the Bald Head was dismantled. Bankers was the front man; it couldn't go on without him as it was his band. I respected his desire to do something different but I didn't like the way he ended things. I was off-island one day and when I returned I was supposed to rehearse with the guys – we always practised at Bankers' house in Buckley's, near to Swetes. But on this day I was tired from the travelling and called Bankers to say I wasn't going. Two hours later Richie called me and said, 'Big Bad Dread and the Bald Head mash up', which is our way of saying it's no more. I felt that after seven years of playing music together, family sacrifices and friendship we deserved a better explanation. But we never got it until we learned about his political aspirations. I am sure it was no coincidence that he dismantled the band after I delivered him a letter from all of us, which expressed our grievances about how he was running things. We hoped he would call a meeting and discuss the various comments, point by point; rather than do that, he ended the whole thing instead. In hindsight, it was probably for the best because we had quite a few issues with Bankers and his ownership on everything and not listening to us. I tried to quit the band myself on several occasions because of these issues. Some rehearsals became quite heated and I would say, 'I'm done with this', pack up my bass and go home because I can't play music when I am unhappy. Richie and keyboardist Dave Bridgwater would always call me to talk me out of leaving the band and remind me of how far we'd come. One thing I will say about Bankers, though, he was a fine singer and songwriter and it was clear he would take some replacing. There was no lasting animosity and the friendship still remains.

The rest of us decided we wanted to carry on and we came up with a new name – Spirited. I was not sure about the new name, though, and felt it sounded a bit lonely on its own. But the name stuck and we formed in January 2009. We left all the old equipment with Bankers and started again with new gear and a new business understanding. We have ambitions to record our own songs and slowly move away from cover versions, which we mostly tend to play on our resident gig nights on Friday and Saturday nights. We have very strong reggae influences but also play calypso (obviously) and other genres. Our singer is a younger lady by the name of Tamah Boston who attracts a different generation. My songs are more old-school!

There are six owners of the band but we're like one big family. It's a professional business. As well as myself (nicknamed 'Long Man' in this band) and Richie, the other four owners are Dave Bridgwater, who is also our musical director and keyboardist, Murphy 'Bumpy' Charles, our percussionist, who also runs his own chauffeuring business, drummer Jason 'Jahson' Jacobs (who drives a grading lorry for the Antigua Public Works) and the band's manager, Tracy Guerrero, an Englishwoman who moved to Antigua many years ago. When Richie and myself are away on tour with the West Indies or other business we are replaced by Carlos, the stand-in guitarist, and Vaughn, who stands in for me on bass. Devon 'Bugs' Emanuel also used to be a part of our band, and was something of a versatile musician who was able to play guitar, bass and drums, and actually helped me out with my bass quite a lot. He still fills in for us whenever called upon. We're a decent sized crew that also includes our sound engineer Karil Knight and backing singer Terry 'Suzuki' Joseph. We're an ambitious band and one can only hope that we continue to grow musically and, who knows, commercially.

For now we're happy to play gigs for the many holiday-makers, especially from the UK, and casual tourists. We're even booked up for weddings. They hire our band to play and the bride may want to have a dance with me or Richie so we have good fun. Primarily we are a working band but we don't mind chilling after and talking cricket with the people in the crowd. Our status does give the band a certain kind of fame but I have never liked getting gigs just because myself and Richie are members with a profile. However I have reluctantly come to accept this is the way it is.

Stanford

'He loved the sound of '20/20 for 20' . . . The Legends were never happy about that and we were all in agreement that we should offer a much lesser prize, maybe $3 million to the winning team . . . $20 million to one team was pure madness'

'Sir' Allen Stanford, as he was known before the Antiguan government took his knighthood away, may well be one of America's most notorious financial criminals, but to Antiguans he was for a long time regarded as a good man who gave many people jobs through his business empire that included banks, an airline, restaurants, his own cricket ground in Coolidge right next to the airport, and more. I never got to know him personally. To me working with him was just about work and business. If we ever bumped into each other away from cricket, he would usually say, 'Hey, Ambi, what's up?' There was nothing more to our relationship than that. To those of us who became involved with his cricket revolution, he appeared to be a man with good intentions and we were happy to work with him, long before he was eventually jailed for 110 years for fraudulent activities. Remember, Allen Stanford had been living in Antigua for many years, employed something like 500 people and was possibly the second biggest employer in Antigua after the government. I had never met him until the Stanford T20 tournament.

When I got the call to be a part of his board of Legends, I liked the concept that was sold to me. I joined Gordon Greenidge, Desmond Haynes, Garfield Sobers, Everton Weekes, Wes Hall, Lance Gibbs, Joel Garner, Courtney Walsh, Andy Roberts, Viv Richards, Richie Richardson, Clive Lloyd, Ian Bishop (who later left due to his media commitments) and Michael Holding, who also later resigned. I don't know Mikey's reasons for resigning but I don't think he ever liked Stanford too much. I remember in one meeting he really got stuck into Stanford. It became a heated discussion between the two of them and Mikey really let him have it. I don't know where all that generated from. Stanford was on the back foot trying to defend much of his vision but Mikey resigned just after that. The board meetings, which were held upstairs at the Sticky Wicket restaurant within the grounds of the Stanford Cricket Ground, usually lasted one or two hours. It was serious business, though he was never tense and he chaired them very casually, though that is not to say there were never any disagreements from both sides, because there were. Clearly, though, as happens when old team-mates get together, there was a fair bit of reminiscing between the Legends. And Stanford always enjoyed listening to stories from the old days, which were normally shared before and after the meetings.

Stanford's vision was about taking cricket further around the Caribbean but, more than that, to try and revive West Indies cricket. At the time our cricket was on a downward spiral and spectators were staying away. Our cricket was going in the wrong direction. So the concept of trying to regenerate interest was a good idea. Stanford explained to us that he had seen West Indies at their best in the 1980s and was now seeing them struggling and this T20 tournament was his way of doing something to address that decline. He claimed to know something about the history of West Indies cricket and appeared passionate about improving the falling interest so I and all of the Legends who were approached bought into his vision.

It wasn't all smooth sailing. There were detractors who felt that as Legends we should not be getting involved with Stanford. The Bajans were the most vocal and some people there suggested we had sold out. They weren't for it and were especially up in arms that the Bajan Legends such as Sir Gary (Sobers), Sir Everton (Weekes), Desi, Joel Garner and Gordon had joined Stanford. They weren't alone in the Caribbean and there were other territories not too happy but the Bajan public were the most vocal in their opposition to this initiative. I don't think they quite grasped what it was all about but maybe they were influenced by the critics who felt it was one big charade and was never going to work. They were generally negative about it. There were other people, too, who were supportive of the concept. We as the Legends always knew what we wanted to achieve so we came on board. The goal for us was simple: to have a more positive effect on West Indies cricket.

The tournament started off very well in July 2006 and grew

in popularity as we took the game around the region. Even some of those doubters jumped on board and admitted the Stanford concept seemed to be a good one after all. The crowds were healthy and the tournament started to progress. Every nation in the Caribbean that had a cricket team was involved, whether it was St Maarten, Montserrat or Turks and Caicos. It wasn't just the usual teams like Barbados, Jamaica and so on. That was an exciting and unique innovation. The first year's tournament was very successful. Players we hadn't been aware of all of a sudden had their opportunity to impress on the big stage. Kieron Powell from Nevis was flying below the radar and the Stanford T20 brought him to light. There were others, too. The whole idea was a good one and it unearthed a lot of talent. Eventually we seemed to have the backing of the masses and the people couldn't wait for the next one. The idea was working well.

We staged another tournament in January 2008, and the growing popularity was evident when I heard that the global television ratings numbered 300 million viewers. But instead of continuing to build on this success and stabilise what was a good tournament that had been working well, Stanford's big ideas took over. He told us he wanted to form a Stanford International XI that would play other international teams. He was quite clear that this side would in no way be dressed up as a West Indies XI. The Legends were to be the selectors and we would have coaches like an international set-up. We made Eldine Baptiste coach, with Roger Harper as his assistant and Lance Gibbs as the manager as we felt one of the Legends should be manager.

Stanford agreed with some things and disagreed on other aspects. If he disagreed on everything it would never have worked. Ultimately he made his own decisions on the way he wanted his tournament to run. Some might suggest we should have walked out or resigned our position on the Legends board because he disagreed with key elements on which we were advising him. But it wasn't a case that he never listened. We were comfortable working with him. He was not a dictator; he always listened to our thoughts and ideas and gave us respect. If he hadn't listened, become dictatorial or disrespected us, I would have resigned right away and I'm sure other Legends would have, too. It is true, though, there were some major decisions that we opposed.

First, Allen Stanford favoured a five-year deal with England worth $100 million. We Legends didn't like that idea. We felt that having England as the same opponents over that period would eventually make things turn a little stale. We told him as much; maybe two years with England would be enough. We thought the West Indies fans should be excited about which team would be visiting next, which would never have been the case with an England XI for five years. We suggested an Australian team after England, then an Indian side, a South African side and so on. We also suggested triangular and quadrangular series. We thought if we ran it like that the supporters would be waiting anxiously as to which team would be coming next; rather than thinking, 'Oh, OK, England again, so what?' But Stanford was really set on having England for five years. We could not talk him out of that concept. And we all know what happened. The ECB went for it. I was one of the Legends along with Viv, Richie and Sir Everton who flew on to the Lord's outfield by helicopter with Stanford for the unveiling, while Sir Ian Botham was also there. I wasn't surprised the ECB officials were taken in by him; we all were. His vision to improve West Indies cricket by using England and, in time, other international teams to help regenerate cricket in the region seemed a hard one to argue with. It disappointed the Legends because we hoped that we were on the Stanford board to be listened to. We knew he would dictate matters as regards business and the money side of things but we were there to guide him on the cricket side. This was partly a cricket decision but what could we do? It's his money and his tournament.

We clashed again over his innovation for the '20/20 for 20', which translated to a one-off Twenty20 match with $20 million for the winner. We told him we didn't have a problem with the guys not being worth the money – that wasn't the issue – but we felt the budget should be a fair bit lower; similar to what had been done with the regional Stanford tournament, which saw the winning team collect $1 million and $500,000 to the runners-up. We knew the budget had to be more than that if we were dealing with international teams but we told him that $20 million was way too much and that he should start lower and increase it every year. But there was no talking him out of it. He loved the idea and loved the sound of '20/20 for 20' – he was hooked on the marketing power of the prize money and knew it would make a big splash in the cricket world. The Legends were never happy about that and we were all in agreement that we should offer a much lesser prize, maybe nearer $3 million to the winning team, then $4 million, $5 million and onwards. Twenty million dollars to one team was pure madness; as with having the same opposition every year, people would know the prize money each year and the novelty value of the $20 million would be lost after Year 1 anyway.

Another concept we didn't like was that of 'the winner takes all'. We felt that was unfair because in this kind of tournament one team must win and one team must lose. We thought the losers must be paid something when we were dealing with international cricketers – it was a minimum expectation. Stanford came back at us with 'But if we reward the losers then none of the players will try hard to win if they know they are going to get well paid anyway, win or lose.' I told him he was talking nonsense. It showed he didn't know much about cricket. When you have prize money of that magnitude everyone is going to want to go out and win it – you will get top-quality cricket. We couldn't persuade him otherwise and it demonstrated his ruthlessness in business. He was a big American tycoon who didn't care much for losers. It was like, if you're a winner in life then good on you. You deserve your huge pay cheque; if you're a loser, bad luck.

I never suspected anything untoward about Stanford – had no reason to while I dealt with him on a purely cricketing basis. I hoped his cricket experiment would continue to flourish. But once the investigations into his business empire began, the whole thing fell apart overnight. Hearing of all the allegations about his fraudulent activities was a bit of a shock. I had never heard anything like it prior to then. It was disappointing because the tournament was doing well and I genuinely believe it would have had some positive impact on West Indies cricket in time. Instead we had people suggesting that we Legends would see our names and reputations dragged down through our association with him. I just laughed at that crap. How could any of us be associated with what he did in his private life or in his other business interests? We dealt with him purely about West Indies cricket so there's no reason why our names should be stained by the collapse of Stanford's cricket initiative. He has proclaimed his innocence but we know he's been found guilty. His innocence or guilt is not for me to judge. My mission along with my fellow Legends was to revive West Indies cricket and it was rather sad that it all ended that way as we were seeing some progress. We need to find other ways and means now to get West Indies cricket back to where it was, at the top of world cricket. However we do that, it is going to take a huge effort on the part of the WICB, the territorial boards, coaches, the players and potential sponsors.

The Greats According to Me

'Wasim Akram was possibly the greatest . . .
He had it all and was the complete package'

My greatest (Test) team – or 13 – is selected from players I've either seen or played against. That rules out greats such as Sir Donald Bradman and Sir Garfield Sobers and many others, but the idea of this exercise is for it to reflect my personal favourite players or those I respected the most as an opponent. Another rule I imposed on myself is not to pick West Indies players as I feel there have been so many greats from my generation it would have been impossible to separate them, with the exception of an obvious three – Malcolm Marshall, Brian Lara and Sir Vivian Richards. I left out many greats. I considered Aravinda de Silva, who I regarded as a very fine player, and the likes of Allan Border and Javed Miandad, but when selecting these kinds of teams you can't name everyone. I didn't nominate a captain but there are several who led their country so this would not be a problem.

SUNIL GAVASKAR – Probably the greatest opening bat there has ever been. I never played against him but I would have loved to because it would have been a great challenge.

GRAHAM GOOCH – I had some battles with him in both international and county cricket. He was a very stubborn, tough customer, a great player and he is a fitting partner for Gavaskar. In the West Indies dressing room we were well aware of Gooch's ability and what he was capable of. His was a wicket we tried to take as quickly as possible.

JACQUES KALLIS – The best all-rounder I've ever seen. Let's exclude Sir Garfield Sobers because I never saw him play. I saw a lot of Kallis over the years and he was clearly the best of many great all-rounders. I have him just ahead of Sir Ian Botham.

SACHIN TENDULKAR – I knew he was going to be great once I saw him score a century against England in 1990 as a 16-year-old. He remained very humble despite all his records and that is a very impressive quality. I was sorry I didn't play more Tests against him as I would have relished the challenge, especially on his home turf.

RICKY PONTING – A great batsman who I always admired. He was very tough; not afraid to take you on as a fast bowler and be dominant – and he did it with a fair amount of success. Those kinds of players always earned my respect.

STEVE WAUGH – We've had our battles, some of which I have spoken of in great detail in this book. I always respected him for being a tough cricketer and he scored runs against me quite a few times, so he had to be in my team as one of my favourite cricketers.

ADAM GILCHRIST – I never played against him in Test Cricket but he was a great wicketkeeper and a destructive batsman. I would have relished the contest of bowling to him. My approach would have been to keep him quiet and tell him, 'You're going to have to score your runs against someone else'.

SIR RICHARD HADLEE – I never played against him, but I have seen him play and always admired him. I feel he was very under-rated and is not talked about enough when people talk about the best fast bowlers of all-time. He was exceptional.

WASIM AKRAM – Possibly the greatest. He could swing the ball, he could seam the ball off the pitch, he could bowl at high pace when he wanted to. Akram had it all and was the complete package. When West Indies played against him, with Sir Viv, Greenidge, Haynes and the rest, his was a name that was talked about a lot in terms of how we were going to approach him and negotiate his threat because we knew what he was capable of.

SHANE WARNE – He was the greatest leg-spinner I've seen. A great competitor and will win games for you, almost single-handedly. Warne is another who was spoken of many times in our dressing room because we were aware of the dangers he possessed. When his captain needed him to produce in the big games, in the big moments, he always delivered.

GLENN McGRATH – A wonderful, match-winning bowler I admired. He was similar to myself in the way he relied on control and accuracy, preying on batsmen's patience to create wicket-taking opportunities. He had a huge heart and a never-say-die attitude.

SIR IAN BOTHAM – I played against him in county cricket at the back end of his career. By then he wasn't the cricketer we know and remember. I am judging him more for his heyday performances when he was a dynamic game-changer with bat, ball and as a great slip catcher. We West Indians like to entertain and Sir Ian always certainly did that.

DAVID GOWER – I played against him and he was such an elegant batsman. Gower was such an easy-going, laid-back cricketer that whether he made a century or a low score, his attitude never changed too much and that is a good quality to have.

AND MY TWENTY20 CHAMPIONS . . .

As we are now in the Twenty20 era, I wanted to share my best T20 team of the modern era, for whom Twenty20 cricket is or was part of their regular schedule, and also a team from my own days, the pre-Twenty20 times. I am sure the older boys would be more than a match for the current T20 stars.

It was a tough task. I wanted to include Virat Kohli, Matthew Hayden, Adam Gilchrist, Sanath Jayasuriya, Yuvraj Singh and

Umar Gul in the modern XI, and I really wanted to find a place for Kapil Dev in the Pre-T20 team. I know Wasim, Waqar and Kalu played a handful of T20 but in general they missed out on this format. I am also aware that I haven't picked a front-line spinner in the retro team but I am backing these pacers to get the job done. While they are all wicket-takers, I cannot imagine any of them conceding too many, even against this calibre of player. But if needed Viv and Collis could bowl some spin.

It would make for one hell of a series between the sides, and I invite readers to judge who they think has the strongest line-up!

Twenty20 Generation Select XI	Pre-Twenty20 Select XI
1. Chris Gayle	1. Gordon Greenidge
2. Brendon McCullum	2. Ian Botham
3. Jacques Kallis	3. Dean Jones
4. AB de Villiers	4. Viv Richards
5. Kevin Pietersen	5. Clive Lloyd (captain)
6. MS Dhoni (captain / wk)	6. Collis King
7. Dwayne Bravo	7. Imran Khan
8. Shahid Afridi	8. Romesh Kaluwitharana (wk)
9. Shane Warne	9. Wasim Akram
10. Muttiah Muralitharan	10. Waqar Younis
11. Lasith Malinga	11. Joel Garner

Curtly Ambrose statistical overview:

	Tests	ODIs	First-Class	List A
Debut:	1988	1988	1986	1986
Matches:	98	176	239	329
Runs:	1,439	639	3,448	1,282
Highest Score:	53	31*	78	48
50/100	1/0	0/0	4/0	0/0
Average:	12.40	10.65	13.95	11.98
Wickets:	405	225	941	401
Best Bowling:	8-45	5-17	8-45	5-17
Average:	20.99	24.12	20.24	23.83
5w / 10w	22/3	4/0	50/8	4/0

Breakdown of his Test bowling achievements

	Matches	Wickets	Average	Best	5wkt	10wkt
Vs Australia	27	128	21.23	7-25	8	1
(in Aus)	14	78	19.79	7-25	6	1
Vs England	34	164	18.79	8-45	8	2
(in Eng)	20	88	20.77	6-52	3	0
Vs India						
(in WI only)	9	15	38.26	5-87	1	0
Vs New Zealand	4	13	21.30	5-68	1	0
(in NZ)	2	5	22.60	3-64	0	0

Vs Pakistan	14	42	27.85	5-35	1	0
(in Pak)	5	15	25.20	5-35	1	0
Vs South Africa	5	21	18.57	6-34	2	0
(in SA)	4	13	23.76	6-51	1	0
Vs Sri Lanka	3	14	13.57	5-37	1	0
(in SL)	1	3	9.00	3-14	0	0
Vs Zimbabwe					
(in WI only)	2	8	12.50	4-42	0	0

(source: Cricinfo)

Acknowledgements

I would like to thank and acknowledge the help and support I have received over the years from the following people, and apologies to anyone I have overlooked: My mother Hillie, for encouraging me towards cricket – not that I appreciated it back in the early days! The whole of my family, especially my brothers and sisters; My wife Bridget for sharing my good days and bad days from the start of my West Indies career and for taking care of our girls while I was often absent through my cricket commitments; My mentor Hugh Gore; My good friend Ballu who I have known since school; My former boss and friend Maurice Francis; Malverne Spencer; Oswald Steele; Enoch Lewis, who was an early influence on me in the Swetes team and in my debut season with Antigua; And all my captains and team-mates over the years; A special mention must also go to Sir Viv Richards for showing faith in me during my rookie days; My good friends Ian Edwards, Winston and Kenny Benjamin and of course my great friend and bowling partner

Courtney Walsh. Thanks also to Richie Benaud and Steve Waugh for kindly writing forewords for this book.

I would like to acknowledge the contribution of literary agents Robyn Drury and Diane Banks and everyone at Aurum for bringing my story to print. And finally to my collaborator Richard Sydenham – if it wasn't for his encouragement and determination to see my story published, this book would never have happened.

I cannot sign off without acknowledging my wonderful supporters locally, regionally and internationally. Thanks everyone.

Sir Curtly Ambrose

Cricket became a passion of mine from the early 1980s because of the exploits of the West Indies. The way Clive Lloyd's West Indies' (soon to be Viv Richards') played the game captivated and inspired; whether it was the positive stroke-play of Gordon Greenidge and Desmond Haynes, the brutality of Viv Richards and Richie Richardson, or Malcolm Marshall, Michael Holding and Joel Garner's rapid danger with the ball. So to then have the opportunity to assist one of the greats of that era – albeit later into the 1980s – in writing his memoirs was hugely rewarding. More so after countless futile attempts as a rookie journalist chasing Curtly Ambrose's interview when he was a player! Not that this was unusual amongst those who attempted the same. It was a pleasure to work with Sir Curtly throughout the writing process and I am sure readers will appreciate the honesty of his story.

Richard Sydenham
(Collaborator on this book)

Index

Names of countries refer to cricket teams.